Mullen It Over

40 Years "Behind The Mic"

by Mike Mullen

2

Layout, Design and Printing by
Post Printing Company
205 W. Fourth St.
Minster, OH 45865

Published by Greyden Press, LLC
2251 Arbor Blvd.
Dayton, OH 45439

First Printing, 2014

ISBN: 978-1-57074-134-0

TABLE OF CONTENTS

PROLOGUE

When I left my childhood home in Silver Spring, Maryland, a couple of months before my eighteenth birthday to enroll as a freshman at Xavier University in Cincinnati, Ohio, I had no idea about the path my life would take.

Aside from knowing that I was granted a college deferment from the Selective Service draft, and that after college, I'd attempt to follow in my father's footsteps as a U.S. Naval Officer, I was clueless as to my long term plan.

When it came to a possible career, I didn't grow up wanting to be anything in particular, so I didn't yearn to enter a specific field of study.

And, as for my personal life, I had no idea that I would marry Rosemary Bohn of Zanesville, Ohio, in February, 1966, get divorced in late 1980, and then marry Amy Freel of Lima, Ohio, in April, 1981.

Additionally, I had no idea that I'd have two children, Julie and Jeff Mullen, and one stepson, Troy Freel, nor did I have any idea that they would eventually bless me with six beautiful grandchildren – Tori and Drew George; Nate, Rami, and Maggie Mullen; and Liam Freel.

I also had no idea that I'd have a successful career as a

sportscaster in Lima and end up broadcasting more than three thousand high school and college ballgames over a span of forty years.

And, finally, I had no idea that a few days after turning 70, I'd begin the daunting task of writing a book about my life's journey.

I have undertaken this project for three reasons. The first is to leave a permanent document for my children and grandchildren so they can better know and understand their dad and "Pops."

The second is to thank the many thousands of sports fans in Northwest Ohio who listened to and supported my radio broadcasts. My goal is to provide them with anecdotes and behind-the-scenes information collected over time. I hope to provide some insight, especially during my early broadcast years, into what it was like to be the voice of Lima sports during an era when radio was the primary electronic means of obtaining one's daily ration of news, sports, and weather information.

The final reason is a very personal one. As a strong Christian, I believe that the Lord blesses each of us with specific talents, and asks us to use them. It's my belief that my gift was the ability to describe athletic events on the air.

And, just as I've been blessed with the gift of being able to play the piano even though I can't read a note of written music, I've also been blessed with a flair for writing. So, after several years of thinking about this project, I believe that now is the time the Lord has prompted me to show what my life has been, especially during my four-plus decades of sitting "behind the mic."

I'd like to thank all of those who contributed to this book, but especially my wife, Amy, for her patience and understanding during my long hours at the computer, and my friend and editor, John Grindrod, who guided me through the entire process and made sure, among other rhetorical matters, that this college English major's punctuation marks were in the right place.

The Beginning

Had it not been for a chance passenger-train encounter between a newly minted U.S. Navy Ensign and a charming young lady from Cincinnati on a business trip for her employer, there would be no story to tell. As an outgoing and attractive young lady, Mary Verina Brink was one of the first females to earn a position as a traveling sales representative for the Procter and Gamble Company, which calls Cincinnati its home. And, it was on that train trip to Chicago when she first met my father, Robert James Mullen.

The train encounter, the first spark in their relationship, took place sometime in 1941. I don't know the particulars about their courtship, but after their long-distance romance fully ignited, they'd set a wedding date for the day after Christmas, 1942.

My father was a product of Irish-Scotch heritage from Milwaukee, Wisconsin. After a difficult childhood that included several years in an orphanage following the divorce of his parents, he earned a scholarship to the University of Notre Dame, where he majored in German and graduated with honors.

The onset of World War II prompted him to become a U.S.

Naval officer after graduation and to use his fluency in German to function as an undercover intelligence officer among German ex-patriots living in South America. Many years later he would counsel me and prompt me to become a Naval officer rather than go through the Vietnam-era draft. His reasoning was simple. In his words, "In the Navy you get clean sheets once a week."

True to his bloodline as the frugal Scot, he always claimed he chose December 26 as his wedding date because the church would still be decorated for Christmas, thus saving him the expense of flowers. It also happened to be a time when he was on leave from his South American assignment.

My mother was from pure German stock and grew up in the Mt. Auburn area of Cincinnati. Her father was Frank Brink, and her mother was Alma Borgemenke. Mom was an excellent student and a 1940 graduate of Edgecliff College in Cincinnati , an institution originally known as Our Lady of Cincinnati College. It remained Edgecliff College until a merger in 1980 with Xavier University.

Following Bob Mullen and Mary Brink's exchanging their wedding vows at Holy Name Catholic Church in Mt. Auburn on that day after Christmas in 1942, on October 25, 1943, I arrived at 5:24 AM at Jewish Hospital in Cincinnati. The name on the birth certificate reads "Michael James Mullen," for a reason that went back ten months earlier.

Picture my mother and father gathered with the whole Brink family on Christmas day, 1942. There were mom's parents; her brothers, Jack and Frank; her feisty maternal grandmother, affectionately called Grandma Borg by all; and a few uncles, aunts and cousins as well.

As the Christmas gift exchange proceeded, my mom selected a package that was to "Mary" from "Grandma Borg." Be aware that Grandma Borg was well ahead of her years in both her interests and her outlook. She was an avid follower of professional wrestling from its first days on black-and-white TV as well as a diehard Cincinnati Reds fan. Additionally, she was young at heart every moment of her 98 years on this earth.

It took just seconds for Mom to open the package and show the contents to the assembled family. Grandma Borg's gift to her about-to-be-married-the-next-day granddaughter was a beautiful and very sexy black negligee.

Suffice it to say that in 1942, when a young woman was suddenly forced to show the garment she might wear on her wedding night to her assembled family members on Christmas morning, said young woman was quickly and thoroughly embarrassed.

And suffice it to say that as a chivalrous young Naval officer with Irish-Scotch heritage, my dad responded to his betrothed's moment of embarrassment by promptly announcing to this group of future German in-laws, "Just for that, Grandma Borg, my first two kids will be named Mike and Pat."

So, that's why on October 25, 1943, the name "Michael James Mullen" was entered on a birth certificate in Cincinnati, and why some years later, on April 3, 1947, the name "Patricia Ann Mullen" was entered on a second birth certificate in Silver Spring, Maryland.

My city of birth is the direct result of the fact that it was my mother's home city as well as her place of residence while my father was deployed to South America on duty as a U.S. Naval Intelligence Officer.

In early 1944, less than six months after my birth, my father received new orders. His assignment was the Pentagon in Washington, D.C., where he would ultimately complete his tour of active duty in the Navy.

My parents purchased a small home in the then-fledgling suburb of Silver Spring for the princely sum of about 14 thousand dollars. And it was in that small but comfortable home that I would grow up until I left for college some 17 years later.

I must have had a very normal early childhood, because my memories of it are all positive albeit quite limited. My dad made his daily commute to the Pentagon, and my mom did what most moms did in the 1940's. She enthusiastically executed her dual role as housewife and mother to her children.

However, while there are limitations to my childhood memories, they remain salient, colorful recollections in my mind, memories which provide vivid contrast to the black-and-white photos of my Truman and Eisenhower years.

Childhood Memories

I f there is one word to describe the life of a suburban child in the late 1940's, it's the word *play*. My job was to figure out how to occupy time and entertain myself. After all, dad had his work, and mom her household chores and was not going to spend all day keeping me company. There were no video games to divert my attention from my outdoor pursuits.

So, I quickly became interested in any endeavor that involved action. The neighborhood kids would ride bikes or play tag, kick-the-can, and hide-and-seek, or organize games of baseball, basketball or touch football without the "benefit" of any adult intervention as we got older. My backyard, someone else's backyard, or the local school playground were the only venues needed unless weather forced us back inside.

There were no organized team sports for anyone younger than eighth grade, so we figured it out on our own. A basketball playground was only two hundred yards away, and a local Naval Academy prep school three blocks away let kids play on their fields anytime they were not in use.

While it never dawned on me while growing up that someday

I'd describe athletic events on radio for a living, I was drawn to sports right from the start.

I listened to Washington Senator and Washington Redskin games on radio as often as possible. On summer days I'd draw a chalk outline of a home plate on the back wall of our brick garage and spend hours pitching complete games with a tennis ball, either walking or striking out every batter depending upon how accurate I was with each pitch. My childhood pals and I followed the natural flow of the sports calendar as kids of that era tended to do, long before there were AAU coaches telling them that they needed to play a sport year round to excel. We'd play H-O-R-S-E during basketball season and touch football during the fall and, of course, when the Senators were plying their trade at nearby Griffith Stadium, we were on a skinned infield playing sandlot baseball and trying our best to execute our own twin killings.

Life was one big playground until something call "school" came along. In the fall of 1948 I made a rather inauspicious entrance into the world of formal education.

As a Catholic living an average three-wood away from St. Michael's Grade School in Silver Spring, I knew I'd be walking to school each morning. Additionally, I knew that my primary education would be entrusted to the good nuns that made up the entire St. Michael's faculty at that time.

However, kindergarten, which was not a St. Michael's program, was another matter. That meant my parents had to find the nearest public school that offered half-day sessions and had to get me there because there was no school bus transportation for kindergarten students.

I clearly recall my mother taking me to my first day of kindergarten. I also recall being very upset at having to navigate such an unknown world on my own. It was during that first tear-filled walk down the school's main hallway that my three foot tall right eye smacked directly into a three foot high brass handle of an open classroom door. I was the only student in that kindergarten class to take home a black eye as an opening-day souvenir.

My grade school years were quite perfunctory. I was a good

student and good grades came without a great deal of exertion. And, that eight year block actually went by with equal parts of speed and relative tranquility.

The routine was as it is for many children: go to school, come home, do homework, go out to play until dinner, and go to bed. The next day the cycle repeated itself. Of course, in the summertime, the routine was different. I started playing in the morning and didn't stop until mom or dad called me for a meal or until the street lights came on after dinner.

Certainly, 1949 was a highlight year for the Mullens because my dad purchased our first family car, a '49 Chevrolet two-door coupe. Meanwhile, next door, the Hanleys bought the first television set in my neighborhood.

In 1950 the situations reversed themselves. The Hanleys became proud owners of a 1950 Ford, and the Mullens welcomed our Philco TV with its blond cabinet and round screen to 813 Bonifant Street. Our new addition opened up a world I hadn't known, a world occupied by shows like "Howdy Doody," "The Mickey Mouse Club," and "The Ed Sullivan Show."

As many Catholic boys did in the 1950's, I became an altar boy and learned to serve mass. It was a time when all the prayers were in that strange dead language that, to this day, simply refuses to die, Latin. Since I lived so close to the school and church, I was often called to fill in at the last minute for someone who failed to show for his assignment. I'd eagerly volunteer to serve Saturday wedding masses because the bridal party would always tip the altar boys. That was much easier money than the paper route I later worked, delivering *The Washington Post* to neighborhood homes.

Around the age of seven, I was introduced to something that would become a very important part of my life. My father enjoyed listening to classical music and played it on the piano. Somewhere he learned to read music, and he played well as long as he had sheet music in front of him. I remember him continuing his piano training during my childhood by taking private lessons from a teacher in downtown Washington, D.C.

As might be expected, I was gently nudged toward the piano

and began my own lessons. I was enrolled with a local private teacher, and for a couple of months, I did my best to absorb the basic elements of reading music and mastering the finger exercises that went with the training.

However, I quickly tired of the mandatory practice sessions and longed to be back outside playing ball with my friends. I rebelled against the structure of lessons, which included all that sheet music and all those nasty scales.

To my parents' everlasting credit, they did not force me to continue the lessons. While I'm sure they were silently pleased a few years later when I returned to the keyboard with a new-found interest in music, at that moment in time, they allowed me to seek a different path and await a possible rediscovery process.

That rediscovery came three years later. I remember sitting at the piano one day when I was 10 years old. I attempted to play the melody notes for the tune "Happy Birthday." Within minutes, I succeeded at figuring out the correct keys, and actually played a one-note version of the song.

My father was both surprised and pleased with this accomplishment and told me that I had a God-given talent to "hear" music. I could tell what the correct melody notes for a song should be by the way they sounded, and, therefore, didn't need what was written on a piece of sheet music.

From that point on, I developed a passion for listening to various kinds of music and for trying to play what I heard on the piano. It literally took me several years to master the art of making the right hand and left hand work together on a tune. Once that happened, piano playing became one of my biggest hobbies and greatest joys.

When it came time to graduate after eight years at St. Michael's, I was now the eldest of not one but three siblings. You've already met my sister Pat who was born in April, 1947. My brother Tom arrived in August, 1950, and another sister, Mary Jane, joined us in July, 1955. We were a typical family, by no means wealthy but comfortable in our suburban home and a generally happy group.

As is the case with many "oldest" children, my mom and dad expected a lot of me. In a way, parents of that era wanted the oldest of their children to be somewhat of a standard bearer, to provide a template for his siblings. And, of course, two well educated parents wanted a college education for their children, so, when it came to my secondary education, I applied to and was accepted at one of the top Catholic high schools in the area.

Little did I know that in the next four years, my life would be changed forever by one of the worst events that can happen to any child.

An Emotional Adolescence

W hile I have no background or training in psychology, experience has taught me that my mother's death, on July 3, 1958, had a more profound effect on me than I ever imagined. It happened the summer after my freshman year in high school, and while profoundly sad, it was not a surprise.

Mom's medical problems started in 1955 when she was pregnant with her fourth and last child, Mary Jane. During the pregnancy, Mom's speech inexplicably became a bit slurred, and she had trouble controlling her facial muscles. Perplexed, our family doctor referred her to a specialist in neurology. The eventual diagnosis was an inoperable brain tumor.

An attempt to kill the tumor with radiation was the only available medical option in 1955, but, because of the pregnancy, even that treatment wasn't possible until after Mary Jane's birth in July. Sometime after that, mom was hospitalized and was given several large doses of radiation. When she came home, I remember her being weak and bedridden for several weeks. Eventually, however, her speech improved, and some of her strength returned.

As I recall, mom slowly became "mom" again, and my

instinctive fears of having a sick parent gradually receded and were replaced by the normal diversions of a new teen, like playing left field for my eighth-grade baseball team, tending to my *Washington Post* paper route, and eventually heading off to Gonzaga High School, a Jesuit college-prep school in downtown Washington, D.C., named after St. Aloysius Gonzaga.

I don't remember the exact timetable, but after about a two-year period of remission, mom's brain tumor returned in early 1958. However, this time there were no medical options because she had already taken the maximum allowable dosage of radiation. The inevitable eventually took its course, and on the morning of July 3, 1958, dad came into the room where my brother Tom and I shared a bunk bed and told us that mom had died during the night.

Nothing can prepare a fourteen-year-old boy for the death of a parent, even, as in my case, when it didn't come as a surprise. The combination of mom's passing and an unusual high-school experience produced an adolescence that was quite different from most of my peers, and those factors were destined to impact some of my most important decisions later in life.

While most high-school students go through four years of coed schooling with people from their neighborhood, my secondary-education experience was vastly different. Not only did my class consist of 165 males and no females, Gonzaga was located twelve miles from my home, and I was the only student from my neighborhood in the class of 1961. I had no daily coed interaction during high school, and, since my classmates came from all over the D.C. and suburban Maryland-Virginia area and none of us had our own cars, we went our separate ways after school and didn't socialize on weekends.

At the same time, my grade-school buddies had dispersed to much closer public or parochial high schools and quickly formed new friendships. While it certainly wasn't intentional on their part or mine, I became a leisure-time loner through high school pretty much by default.

After eight years of leaving home five minutes before the bell rang for a grade-school building 200 yards away, my high-school days were much more complex. They started at 6:00 AM and lasted until 9:00 or 10:00 PM. During freshman and sophomore years, my route to school included a commuter-train ride from Silver Spring to Washington's Union Station and then a nine-block walk to Gonzaga's front steps at North Capital and I streets. My route home involved a minimum of three car rides and took anywhere from one to two hours, depending on the generosity and destination of drivers who routinely picked up high-school hitchhikers.

My school transportation options improved during my junior and senior years because I found a man in our neighborhood who worked just two blocks from the school. I would ride in with him in the morning and ride home with him when he got off at 5:00 PM. That gave me time after school to get involved with activities like the school newspaper and the debating society.

It also meant I didn't get home from school until nearly 6:00 PM each evening. And, since I rarely had fewer than three hours of homework, I went straight to my bedroom desk after dinner and hoped to finish my assignments before a 10:00 PM bedtime. There were no phone calls and no television, just a top-40 radio station playing in the background as I studied.

Sports were a big deal at Gonzaga, and I loved following the teams even though I wasn't talented enough to play. However, I contributed to the sports scene by writing a sports column for the school newspaper. The name of the column was "Mullen It Over," a name I could never have guessed at that time would be put back to good use some 25 years later at WIMA Radio in Lima.

My Gonzaga Eagles played football in the Catholic School League (CSL), and at the end of the season, the CSL champ would play the public-school champ for the city title at Griffith Stadium, the home of both the Washington Senators and Washington Redskins. My junior year, our football team won the city championship 7-6, when our best player, senior Jon Morris, blocked the potential tying extra-point kick late in the fourth quarter. Morris was a three-sport star at Gonzaga. He enjoyed a standout career as a center and linebacker at Holy Cross University, and went on to play eleven years at center for the Boston/New England Patriots before rounding out a truly noteworthy fifteen-year professional career with the Detroit Lions and Chicago Bears. Morris was a seven-time all-star and was the first Patriot selected to a Pro Bowl after the AFL and NFL merged in 1969.

Griffith Stadium also provided the backdrop for another interesting high-school experience. During the 1959 and 1960 NFL seasons, I was hired as a concession-stand attendant for Redskin home games. These were the days before the automated soft-drink dispensers we see today in any fast-food restaurant. If someone ordered four Cokes, for example, one of us had to dip an arm into a very cold ice chest, dig out four bottles, uncap them, and then pour each bottle's contents into a paper cup. Do that for three or four hours on a bone-chilling November Sunday, and your dominant arm will approach a condition just short of frostbite.

Sixteen workers were assigned to each concession stand, but only twelve were on duty at a time. Each employee worked three quarters and got to watch the game for one quarter. We'd draw numbers before kickoff to determine the order of "work" and "watch." During those two seasons, the few dollars I earned from this part-time job paled in comparison to the thrills I got listening to the Redskins Marching Band play "Hail to the Redskins" each time the team scored or watching Eddie LeBaron quarterback my favorite NFL team in person. While it was only for one quarter, most other Redskin fans were limited to listening to the games on their living-room radios. The now taken-for-granted "NFL on CBS" each Sunday afternoon was still a network TV executive's pipe dream in the late 50's.

While the Colts-Giants NFL championship game in 1958 is often cited as the turning point for the NFL in terms of its assuming its position as a major player on the American sports landscape, the sport's momentum was gradual.

High-school basketball was equally competitive, especially in the CSL. One of our big rivals was Archbishop John Carroll High School. This school was opened in 1951 by the Augustinian order as the first intentionally integrated high school in Washington, D.C.

This came a full four years before the historic *Brown vs. Board of Education* Supreme Court decision that would make integrated schools the law of the land, and the concept was by no means fully welcomed by D.C. residents.

Bob Dwyer was an insurance salesman who also held the part-time job as boys varsity basketball coach at John Carroll. His superiors asked him to market the idea of an integrated education to young men of all ethnic backgrounds. The goal was to show everyone that a peacefully integrated school was the key to both academic and athletic success.

By the late 50's, Coach Dwyer had done his job very well. His teams between 1958 and 1960 combined to win 55 straight games and captured two consecutive Knights of Columbus Invitational Tournaments held each spring at Georgetown University. This event featured top high-school powers from up and down the Eastern Seaboard such as Power Memorial in New York and Brother Rice in Philadelphia.

The 1958-59 John Carroll team started John Thompson, Jr., at center. It was the same 6'11" John Thompson who starred at Providence College and later became the storied coach at Georgetown University. The forwards were Tom Hoover and Ed "Monk" Malloy. Hoover became a standout player at Villanova. Malloy played at the University of Notre Dame, became a Holy Cross priest, and in 1987, succeeded the legendary Fr. Theodore Hesburgh as president of Notre Dame, a job he would hold until his retirement in 2005.

The guards for the Carroll Lions in '58-'59 also had Division I talent. Walt Skinner went on to a career at Catholic University in D.C., and George Leftwich followed his neighborhood pal, Tom Hoover, to Villanova and led the Wildcats to the NIT title in 1965.

The 1959-60 Carroll starting five was the same as the year before with one exception. Hoover was now a freshman at Villanova, and John Austin took his place at Carroll. Austin eventually starred for Boston Celtic legend Bob Cousy, who became Boston College's head basketball coach after his playing career.

Two full seasons with an entire starting lineup of legitimate Division I college talent certainly made Coach Dwyer's job easier. No wonder the Lions won 55 in a row, including four home-and-away blowout victories over my Gonzaga Eagles.

But their success and acclaim came with a serious personal price. Coach Dwyer received a number of death threats because of his notably interracial lineup, and he once received a call that his daughter would not make it home alive from her grade school the next day if Carroll won its game that evening. Fortunately, none of these threats materialized, and to this day, people like Tom Hoover and George Leftwich credit the classrooms, hallways and athletic venues of John Carroll High School for their subsequent academic and professional success. Leftwich, in fact, returned many years later and served as athletic director at Carroll from 2005 until his retirement in 2013.

As I look back on my high-school experience, I can make the same claim as Hoover and Leftwich about the quality of education that I received at Gonzaga. The Jesuit education was outstanding, and the time went quickly. The days were so filled with bookwork, extra-curricular activities and round-trip travel to and from school that it made dealing with the emotional scars of my mother's death somewhat easier. I was the oldest of four children and expected to set the example that life goes on, so deal with it. Dad was faced with the incredible challenge of finding caretakers for us on weekdays because continuing to work full time at the Pentagon was his only way to support the family.

I recall several women filling the caretaker role in the months following mom's death, but a conversation Dad had with his four children over the Christmas break in 1958 would be the harbinger for another seismic change in the Mullen family.

Our New Mom

O ne of life's immutable axioms is that the job of parenting does not come with an instruction manual. Even when circumstances are as they should be, it's a demanding two-person task. When tragedy took my mom out of the equation, I can only imagine the pressure my dad felt when, in mid-1958, at the age of forty, he found himself a single parent of two boys and two girls, ages 3 through 14.

While a series of housekeepers took care of the weekday chores of cooking, cleaning and making sure we kids didn't kill each other, Dad knew a more permanent solution was needed. So, in relatively short order, his search for a new wife and mother for his children began. However, consider the odds he faced. I doubt many women were interested in dating after hearing an introduction like, "Hi, I'm Bob Mullen, a recent widower with four kids. Would you like to go out to dinner with me Saturday night?"

However, circumstance and, I'm sure, a good dose of divine intervention helped even those odds as events began to unfold that were destined to bring a new woman into our lives.

Doctor Peter Lombard was an ear, nose and throat specialist

in Silver Spring. He saw my mother during the early stages of her illness because his first suspicions were that she suffered from Bell's palsy, a disease that often involves ear discomfort and weakens facial muscles. His office manager was a young woman named Anne Herzig. Anne was 26 and still single. She became acquainted with the Mullen family through mom's visits to Dr. Lombard and also because my brother Tom was treated in the same office a number of times for ear-infection problems.

Several months after my mom died, her feisty grandmother, the lady we all called Grandma Borg, passed away. Dad felt compelled to attend her funeral in Cincinnati but needed someone to stay with his four children for a couple of days while he was gone. The daily housekeepers weren't an option, so he thought about Anne Herzig. After all, she knew the family and lived just a couple of blocks away. So, he called and asked her if she'd be willing to stay at our home and take care of us while he went to Grandma Borg's funeral.

Knowing the situation that Dad faced and wanting to help, Anne honored his request. When Dad returned from Cincinnati, he took Anne out to dinner as an extra "thank you" for caring for us during his absence.

And, as it turned out, something must have been put into motion that evening, but when Dad soon attempted to ask Anne for another date, he was initially unsuccessful because she deliberately avoided his calls. For Anne, there were many issues to consider, and she didn't want to be in any way impulsive. Age is often a consideration in matters of romance, and, after all, Dad was fourteen years her senior. Also, there were, of course, four other considerations - my brother, two sisters and me. I think in her mind, a thank-you dinner was one thing, but a second-date request that was accepted signaled an interest in a possible relationship.

As she weighed her options and avoided several phone calls, something must have happened because Anne finally said yes to that second date and to others after that, including a request to stop over one evening and help Dad wrap Christmas presents. As far as what may have happened, when it comes to matters of this type of chemistry, a room full of lab coats would be hard-pressed to explain what draws people together who come from such divergent circumstances.

How appropriate it was that exactly one year before the 1959 Broadway musical *Sound of Music* introduced the Von Trapp family to the world, a Von Trapp-like love story was unfolding in Silver Spring, Maryland. Granted, there were no Alps, Mother Abbess, or threatening Nazis, but there was a widowed officer, a young woman who had cared for his children while he was away, a budding romance, and an eventual question to the officer's children on Christmas Eve. And, that question was, for the Mullen children, "How would you like Anne to be your new mother?"

With the kids' vote unanimously affirmative and the potential new mother also in agreement, Anne received an engagement ring in February, 1959, and my father and Anne set a wedding date for the following June. I remember being excited that Anne was joining the family, not so much as "Mom" because her role in my life, at least initially, would take on more that of an older sister than a mother. Perhaps that was because she owned a 1955 Chevy convertible, and I was just months away from my sixteenth birthday. It doesn't get any better than that for a teenage boy!

A Saturday wedding in June was by far the most popular choice for brides in 1959. However, the prospect of finding an open June Saturday at St. Michael's Church in Silver Spring, a scant four months away, wasn't likely. That's why it was on a Monday morning, June 22, 1959, when my dad and Anne Marie Herzig walked down the aisle. Dad, still an officer in the Naval Reserve, was in his dress whites while Anne wore a beautiful white wedding dress. As for me, well, I wore a black cassock and white surplice because, after all, it was a wedding at St. Michael's, so who else would serve as an altar boy that day, right?

Becoming a parent of four children in one day didn't seem to faze our new mom one bit, although she faced very different challenges with her suddenly acquired brood. Mary Jane was a toddler who needed a full-time mom. Tom was almost nine and probably not quite sure of what to make of the whole situation. Pat likely had the most difficulty adjusting because she was twelve and faced transition into womanhood with a new mom she barely knew. In addition, Pat had, at a young age and by necessity, taken on many household chores during her own mother's illness, so she wanted more than anything to just be a kid again. However, during Pat's high-school years, as would become evident soon, she was thrust into an expanded role as "big sister," and I'm sure she bristled more than once when she was assigned tasks like babysitting for a still-growing family.

I probably had the easiest transition because, as I said, at that time, I related to Anne more as an older sister than a mother. She deftly found ways to be my mother without specifically trying to "mother" me. Also, in two short years I would be leaving for college and, therefore, would no longer be involved in the daily schedule of my growing family. And, as for those who might wonder how much bigger Bob Mullen's family could get, well, I went from being the oldest of four to being the oldest of ten in just over eight years!

My first new sister, Kathleen, was born in April, 1960. Christine came in October, 1961. Then there was Maureen in August, 1963, Colleen in June of 1964, and more than three years after the last birth suggested to us that the family was complete, John and Lisa were a "twin" surprise in December of 1967.

Fortunately, Anne took to motherhood seamlessly and, out of sheer necessity, ran the household with the precision of a drill sergeant. One example of organization was her plan for remembering birthdays. Having grown up in Silver Spring and eventually working for Dr. Lombard for several years, she created a network that consisted of many area friends and acquaintances. She had also married into a whole new family, which meant there were distant uncles, aunts, cousins and such, which meant it wasn't unusual for her to have nearly two dozen birthdays to remember and recognize each month.

So, to solve the problem, she wrote each recipient's name on his or her birthday on a special calendar used just for that purpose. Then, on the first day of each month, she wrote and addressed all

3

the birthday cards for that month. She would put the date to be mailed in the corner where the stamp belonged and set the month's pile of cards on a small desk in our kitchen. Each morning, one of the kids was assigned the job of putting a stamp on the cards for that date and taking them to the corner mailbox.

Anne was also an excellent cook. She had learned well from her mother, and she was a master at making meals that were not only tasty but very efficient. She'd often cook enough for two meals and then freeze half so we could enjoy the same meal again a few days later without all the preparation time.

Having a new mother just eleven years older than I was occasionally brought about awkward but comical moments. There was that time in late summer, 1961, just before I left home for college. My new sister, Kathy, was sixteen months old, and mom was about seven months pregnant with Christine. One afternoon I drove the woman who was gradually becoming more Mom than Anne and Kathy to our local Safeway grocery store to pick up a few things for dinner that night. At checkout, the items filled about three-quarters of one brown paper bag. A high-school boy bagged the groceries, and since I was holding Kathy on my shoulder and Mom was obviously quite pregnant, he politely asked if she needed help carrying the bag to her car. Without a second's hesitation, Mom quite innocently said, "Oh no, my son can handle it. Thanks." The look on the teenage bagger's face was priceless. Since I was 17 and she was 28, I'm carrying a baby and she's pregnant, the non-verbal communication basically said, "Sure lady, your 'son' will handle it. Tell me another good one!"

During the time I spent at home after Dad remarried, for all of us kids, Anne became Mom, and more than a half-century later, I believe no one has ever more richly deserved the title. I'm grateful to say that she still holds that honored place in our family to this day.

For the four original Mullen children, having a new mom also meant having new grandparents. Joseph Herzig emigrated from Europe to the United States in 1927 and obtained a job with the Danish Embassy in Washington, D.C. Once established, he brought the love of his life, Amalia (Malka for short), to America, and they married. Their first child, Anne, was born in the spring of 1932. Her sister Dorothy came three years later.

Grandpa Herzig was a man of many talents, and I liked him right from the start. He was a master house painter and could hang wallpaper with the best. He and Malka also made extra money working for a catering company. Malka was an excellent cook, and she and Joe helped cater many parties in the D.C. area.

When Anne joined our family, it was the summer between my sophomore and junior years in high school, which meant I was certainly of working age without threatening any child-labor laws. So, Grandpa Herzig hired his new grandson to work with him painting houses, and I did that for two summers. It was quite an experience. He could paint an entire average-size bedroom with an eight-inch brush in the time it would take me to paint the trim on one window in the same room.

Most paint in the late 50's was oil based as opposed to the nearly universal latex paints used today, and, since rollers were not yet in vogue, brushes were used for all jobs. That meant after eight hours of painting, we would spend at least another hour at the end of the day cleaning these professional-grade brushes with turpentine and rags so that they would be ready to use again. While my dad always modeled a strong work ethic during my life, those two summers with Grandpa Herzig put an exclamation point on the importance of working hard, doing a professional job, and being responsible for my own success.

As my senior year in high school approached, it was time for me to think about college, and the recipe that went into my decision had three ingredients. First, I wanted to go away to school, but I also wanted some sense of familiarity. Second, growing up, I spent many two-week summer vacations in Cincinnati, and I carried fond memories of great times at Coney Island with my Brink cousins and of seeing the Reds play each summer at Crosley Field. And, third, since both of my mother's brothers were graduates of Xavier University in Cincinnati, it was a natural for me to want to follow in their footsteps.

So I applied, and when Xavier offered me a half-tuition academic scholarship based on my high-school grades, I quickly accepted and knew that for the next four years, if I needed a meal on weekends, Grandma Brink's house wasn't far away.

Off To College

My four years at Xavier University in Cincinnati, from 1961 to 1965, included a wide variety of experiences, but, as my path would ultimately unwind, none factored into my future career in radio. I lived in the same house located a couple of blocks off campus from start to finish. Additionally, I also earned a sports letter, something I never did in high school. And, perhaps more impacting, I experienced the dark side of the civil-rights struggle first hand as part of a student-exchange program with a school in Mississippi. Even though my sights were set on joining the Navy, I also took part in the school's Army ROTC program. Oh, and by the way, I also met the woman I would eventually ask to be my wife.

Xavier mirrored my high-school experience at Gonzaga in two important ways. First, both schools were run by the Jesuits, and, second, both had male-only student bodies. While women were accepted in the graduate school at Xavier in the early 60's, none were enrolled as undergraduates.

My academic goals in college were to earn a bachelor's degree in English and minor in history and philosophy. I chose a liberal-arts curriculum because I had no interest in science, math or business. Attending college entitled me to "deferment" status with the Selective Service, but I knew that status would end upon graduation. And, since I had no desire to become an infantry soldier with a likely deployment to the most potentially lethal war zones in Vietnam, my sole post-college goal was to qualify for the Navy's Officer Candidate School (OCS) in order to avoid being drafted into the Army.

In the early 1960's, housing options at Xavier ranged from traditional on-campus dormitories to a few off-campus houses for students with similar extracurricular interests. I don't remember the circumstances, but I was assigned to one of the off-campus residences called the Sodality House.

The building was an old three-story mansion, no doubt, at one time a house of grandeur for one of Cincinnati's wealthy, if only those walls could have spoken to us. However, during my time, Sodality House was the school-year home for thirty young men who all came from similar Jesuit high-school backgrounds. Two doors down the street was a house called the Clef Club, where many members of the Xavier choir lived. Another residence on the same street was Knights Manor, which was affiliated with and supported by the local Knights of Columbus.

While casual observers might understandably think Sodality House was like a traditional Greek fraternity residence found on most state school campuses, there was actually little similarity. There was never a "rush" to recruit new members because there was no organization to join. We were simply a group of students seeking two things not readily available in the dorms. We wanted a generally quiet place to study and an alternative to a steady diet of cafeteria food. We did our share of partying, but it was rarely at the house. Since there were no female undergraduates to impress and since Ohio law permitted anyone 18 and older to purchase beer with 3.2 percent or less alcohol content, "party time" usually involved chugging down a cold Hudepohl or two about ten o'clock at night with a few housemates at Woody's, a small restaurant and bar located just one block away. A couple of trips per week to Woody's after hitting the books used up what meager spending money I had.

My room for all four years was the original first-floor kitchen. It contained a set of bunk beds, two desks, an old porcelain kitchen sink, and a door that led out to the back porch. I liked it because it was small, easy to keep clean, and enough out of the way of main-house traffic to be a quiet place to study. A Cleveland St. Ignatius grad, Bill Masterson, was my roommate all four years. Bill and two other Sodality House guys from Cleveland, Terry Rohen and Terry Wallace, became good friends, but the relationships withered after college, in large part I believe, because there was no "social media" way to keep in touch at the time, and our lives went in four very different directions.

Sodality House had a housemother, a middle-aged widow named Mrs. Schick, who lived at the house on weekdays and cooked the evening meals. Each student in the house was assigned one night per week to set the tables for dinner and, afterward, to wash, dry and put away the dishes. One night of "KP" a week was more than worth the value of great home cooking. On weekends, Mrs. Schick went to her own home, and we either did our own cooking, ordered in pizza, or, in my case, headed to Grandma's house for a meal.

In the spring of my freshman year, I saw a notice on the bulletin board in the student union inviting anyone interested in joining the Xavier tennis team to come out to practice. I had played recreational tennis during high school and enjoyed the sport, so I showed up on the date and time indicated. While tennis wasn't a scholarship sport at Xavier in the early 60's, the coach had to fill six singles' positions and three doubles' teams in order for us to compete with other schools in a typical nine-match college event.

I'm not sure if it was because of talent or because so few showed up to try out, but I was chosen to play number-six singles and number-three doubles. We Musketeers held our own against schools where tennis was also just a club sport, but scholarship opponents were another story. Our schedule called for an away match at Kentucky. Since scholarship players made up the entire

Wildcats' roster, suffice it to say, it took us longer to drive the seventy miles from Cincinnati to Lexington than it did for us to lose all nine matches.

Despite our occasional doses of reality when we faced scholarship-laden opponents, I was proud to play tennis at Xavier, since it provided me with both my first and last college letter. I played for only one season because better talent became available and because I took a part-time job working twenty hours per week in the Alumni Office at Xavier.

My primary pre-computer-era task was to operate a machine that made metal plates, about the size of military dog tags, for use in the office addressograph machine. As I typed, letters and numerals of the names and addresses of Xavier alumni were punched into the metal plates. The plates were then placed in alphabetical order into trays. When the university sent a mass mailing to alumni, one tray at a time was inserted into the addressograph machine. The machine then automatically stamped an envelope or label with the address of each plate in the tray. Even in the 60's, Xavier had several thousand alumni, so with the addressograph machine, we could address envelopes or labels for the entire group in about ninety minutes. It would have taken days to do the same job using regular typewriters. I worked in the Alumni Office for three years, and the job helped pay my way through school and keep me in beer money for those weeknight visits to Woody's.

The major sports of football and men's basketball were big during my time at Xavier. Our hoops team had several classic battles with the University of Cincinnati when the Bearcats were a national power and featured players like Ron Bonham, Tom Thacker and Tony Yates. Xavier currently plays in the beautiful Cintas Center on campus, but the Musketeers' home court in the early 60's was the cozy-but-small Schmidt Fieldhouse. UC also had a relatively small home court at the time, Armory Fieldhouse, so the schools agreed to play each other on a neutral court at the more commodious Cincinnati Gardens to accommodate the cross-town rivalry crowd. In one of those matchups, Xavier guard Steve

Thomas scored 45 points against Yates when Yates was thought by many to be the national defensive player of the year, but it wasn't quite enough as my Musketeers fell 94-92.

As far as the fall sport that today captivates so many college campuses, Xavier shut down its football program after the 1973 season because it had been losing six-figure money for several years. However, in the early 60's, for many, games were must-see Saturday events. The Musketeers played on campus at Corcoran Stadium, which opened in 1929 and held 15,000 people. The stadium was eventually demolished in 1988 and the site now contains the Xavier soccer field.

I especially remember the times we'd pull an all-nighter at the Sodality House on the Friday before Homecoming making our float for the parade. And for each home game, those who attended from the house would sit as a group and cheer on the Musketeers.

Xavier football was coached for eight years in the 60's by Ed Biles, who later served as an assistant coach for several NFL teams and succeeded Bum Phillips as head coach of the Houston Oilers from 1981-83. Though the season records hovered around .500 under Biles, the Musketeers routinely sent one or two players to the NFL each year. One standout I remember was Danny Abramowicz, a 1967 graduate, who enjoyed an eight-year career with the New Orleans Saints and was one of the top receivers in the league.

The early 60's were a volatile time in the United States with respect to the civil-rights movement and the integration of college campuses. As a Catholic university, Xavier welcomed black students and sponsored several programs during the year encouraging educational integration. One program featured a student-exchange with Tougaloo College, an all-black Christian school in Jackson, Mississippi. Because I was curious to learn more about the topic, and, more importantly, the world around me, I volunteered for the program.

A classmate of mine who had relatives in Jackson helped set up the exchange, which took place just before Christmas break during my sophomore year. He drove himself, me, and two other

white students from Cincinnati to Mississippi to spend three days
on the Tougaloo campus. At the same time, four black students
from Tougaloo came to Cincinnati to complete the exchange on
Xavier's campus.

Although I'm sure I fashioned myself to be as worldly as all
college students view themselves, I soon learned that I wasn't at
all prepared for the experience. When it quickly became known
that some northern "white college boys" were in town and staying
in the black dorms at Tougaloo, we were watched like hawks. One
gas station in Jackson refused to sell us gas because our car bore
Ohio license plates, and, certainly, the word was out about why we
were in town.

There was a white physician at a Jackson hospital who was
sympathetic to the civil-rights movement. When he learned that
four students from Ohio were at Tougaloo to learn first-hand about
school integration, he wanted to meet, share his perspective on the
issue, and, perhaps, see if we could be of help in the future. For his
personal safety, however, the doctor set up the meeting at a remote
location well out of town, had us come in two different cars from
different directions, and didn't even tell his wife or kids about
the meeting for fear that an innocent remark in the wrong place
might expose him as someone in favor of school integration. Such
exposure would have cost him his job and may have brought harm
to his family.

It didn't take long in that setting before I felt like the triple-
agent character of Herb Philbrick in the mid-50's TV spy series
I Led Three Lives. The people at Tougaloo were very nice and
gave us no reason to fear. We were taken to a men's basketball
game against another all-black school and thoroughly enjoyed a
contest that saw both teams score more than one hundred points.
But the Tougaloo hospitality could not mask the reality that most
people in Jackson feared any out-of-state whites who chose to mix
educationally with blacks, and they wanted us gone as soon as
possible.

In fact, on the morning our Jackson classmate drove us to the
airport to catch flights home for Christmas, a local sheriff's cruiser

came speeding up behind the car and pulled us over for no legal reason at all. After the sheriff verified that we were the suspicious students from Ohio, he told us through the driver's lowered window, in no uncertain terms, that Yankee college rabble-rousers weren't welcome in Jackson, and to "get the hell out of town and don't come back." I was more than happy to leave, but I was glad for the chance to learn first-hand about the virulent opposition to school integration in the Deep South.

As part of my experience at Xavier, I elected to take part in the two-year Army ROTC program offered on campus. Since I knew that I'd be applying for a Navy OCS billet after graduation, I figured having some military training on my resume would help my chances. So during my sophomore and junior years, I took classes in military history and learned to execute procedures like field-stripping, cleaning and reassembling an M-1 rifle. The training also included target practice on the range in the ROTC building. While I could have never known this at the time, as it turned out, this remains the only time in my life that I've ever fired a rifle.

My social life in college centered around an occasional date with a girl from one of the local Catholic colleges or one of the nursing students at Good Samaritan Hospital in Cincinnati. Often a bunch of guys would attend the organized "mixers" on the Xavier campus, where girls from the local schools were also invited to attend.

I continued to develop my piano playing with the help of a housemate who took lessons at the Cincinnati Conservatory of Music and played with a trio at a local jazz club on weekends. I also learned to play the guitar and teamed up with another guitar-playing housemate, my friend Terry Wallace, plus a local female singer, to form a campus folk group called "The Axmen." We were a poor-man's version of Peter, Paul and Mary and played just for fun and, once in a while, a couple of beers at local parties.

In the spring of my junior year, as best I recall, The Axmen were invited to perform at a weekend folk festival on the campus of St. Mary of the Woods College in western Indiana. There were students from several schools in Ohio, Indiana and Michigan represented, and it was during that weekend that I met a girl from Zanesville, Ohio, named Rosemary Bohn. We hit it off right from the start and even learned that we shared the identical birthday of October 25, 1943.

She attended a school in Columbus now known as Ohio Dominican University. At that time, however, it was the College of St. Mary of the Springs, a school that had been chartered in 1911 as an all-women's college. We traveled back and forth to see each other a few times during the late spring and summer of 1964, before settling down in Cincinnati and Columbus for our respective senior years.

Because our schools were a hundred miles apart, our relationship developed primarily over the telephone and through letters. We gradually fell in love and, following the trend set by most young Catholics in the mid-60's who were cautioned from an early age about the dangers and sinful nature of pre-marital sex, we decided to get married as soon as possible after college.

In June, 1965, I graduated *magna cum laude* from Xavier with a degree in English. While I presumed the next chapter in my life would involve the United States Navy, Uncle Sam had other ideas.

Anchors Aweigh

A degree with honors from Xavier in June, 1965, and two years of ROTC training formed a resume that I presumed would ensure my acceptance into the U.S. Naval Officer Candidate School (OCS) in Newport, Rhode Island. I truly felt that my acceptance would be little more than a formality and that I'd be heading east by the end of that summer.

The acceptance letter arrived less than a month after I applied, but my class reporting date of August, 1966, was a total shock. OCS was a busy four-month curriculum and, at that time, the school started a new class of five hundred candidates each month. I had no idea that the application backlog was so large that I'd have to wait thirteen months to start the process.

The challenge now was to find a way to support myself for a year before entering the service. Teaching at a Catholic grade school was both a viable and available option. At the time, Catholic grade schools didn't pay as much as public schools, but their only professional requirement was a college degree, whereas public schools demanded specific college training in elementary education.

St. Michael the Archangel Grade School in Sharonville, a northern suburb of Cincinnati, had an opening for a seventh-grade teacher that fall, and I was more than happy to accept the position, given the fact that a small paycheck was certainly better than none. My contract required me to teach every subject except religion, which then was still the domain of the nuns and parish priest. I was fine with English and history. Math was not my forte, but my skills were certainly sufficient enough for the subject on a seventh-grade level. As for science, I didn't understand half the chapters in the textbook but did my best not to thwart the progress of any budding scientists in the class.

With a transitional job in place and a slot secured at OCS for the following summer, Rosemary and I set a wedding date for February of 1966 in Zanesville. I purchased my first new car, a green 1965 Volkswagen Beetle, for just over $1700.00. Upon graduation from Xavier, I rented an apartment in Mt. Adams, an eclectic neighborhood overlooking downtown Cincinnati, and, after the wedding, that became our first home.

Our initial months together were typical of most newlyweds. We went to work each day, dined out occasionally with friends, and also managed to succumb to the persuasive show-and-tell performance of a door-to-door salesman who sold us an overpriced Rainbow vacuum cleaner that we didn't need just because it used a clear-plastic reservoir of water instead of a bag to trap whatever was lurking in our carpet. It's amazing how dirty a gallon of water looks after two minutes of vacuuming an old shag carpet, and Rosemary and I invested heavily into the visual of all that dirty water.

When it came time to report to Officer Candidate School in mid-August, 1966, Rosemary was pregnant with our first child. Since OCS students weren't allowed to leave base for the first two months of training, Rosemary stayed in Cincinnati until late October. During the final two months at OCS, we were allowed time off from Saturday morning until Sunday evening. Once I could finally see her on weekends, Rosemary came to Newport and rented a second-floor apartment in a local home.

My time at OCS turned out to be the most intense four months of my life. It was a combination of boot camp and graduate school. Each candidate was assigned to a company named after the Navy term for a letter of the alphabet, such as Alpha, Bravo and Charlie. I was assigned to November Company and vividly recall lying in my bunk the first night in the barracks and saying to myself, "What the hell did I get myself into?"

Each day was packed with demanding physical training, information about Navy customs and traditions, and very difficult courses that covered the broad scope of information I would need to function as an officer aboard ship. Several young men in my class washed out in less than a week. I survived and was named November Company commander for the final month of the school.

I completed my OCS training and received a reserve-officer commission as a U.S. Navy ensign in mid-December, 1966. Since Rosemary was due just three weeks later, the Navy was kind enough to assign me three months of temporary duty aboard a destroyer based in Newport. This allowed our daughter, Julie, to be born at the base hospital on January 6, 1967, and gave us a couple of months to get settled with a newborn before it was time for me to carry out my permanent orders. Those required me to travel to the U.S. Naval Base at Pearl Harbor, Hawaii, and report for duty as the communications officer aboard the *USS Davidson*. The ship was just over a year old and one of a new class of destroyer-escorts, thus its hull bore the number DE-1045. It was 414 feet long, carried a complement of 15 officers and 180 enlisted men, and was outfitted with the latest in anti-submarine warfare technology.

In late March, 1967, Rosemary and I packed our few earthly possessions for shipment and then, with a bassinette wedged into the backseat for Julie, took off in the Beetle on a cross-country trip from Newport to San Diego, California. There, the Navy issued us plane tickets to Honolulu, and we arrived the first week of April.

I was aware that my ship was scheduled for a lengthy deployment to Vietnam soon after I reported aboard, and "soon" turned out to be less than a week, so there wasn't really time to get the family settled. Five days after I arrived in Hawaii, the *Davidson* along with the rest of our destroyer squadron and the aircraft carrier *Constellation* pulled away from Bravo Pier in Pearl Harbor and set sail for the South China Sea.

The next six-months-plus would be incredibly challenging for both Rosemary and me. She had to quickly adapt to military life and handle all the details of moving into base housing while at the same time being a new mother and now single parent of a three month old. I had to quickly absorb the myriad details of shipboard life, from standing watch both on the bridge and in the Combat Information Center to running a 25-man division that included radiomen, signalmen, and the ship's postal clerk.

Deployment stories could fill another book, but I'll summarize the experience. Our mission was to escort the *Constellation*, protect it and other ships from possible submarine attack, and serve as a rescue ship for pilots during flight operations should a plane malfunction while taking off from or returning to the carrier. My life for 26 weeks boiled down to eating, sleeping, and standing watch. The only free time was occasional liberty in the Philippine Island port of Subic Bay and a three-day stay in Hong Kong. And, since the Internet and cell phones were not yet invented, the only way to communicate with my wife and family was through letters, which often arrived, at either end, weeks after we wrote them. Needless to say, I was more than ready for the day in late October, 1967, when our carrier group completed the deployment and sailed back into Pearl Harbor.

I remained stationed aboard the *Davidson* for eighteen months. During the year following deployment, other than an occasional multi-day training exercise at sea, and my every-fourth-day duty overnight aboard ship, I worked normal business hours and went home after work.

My son Jeff was born at the base hospital in Honolulu on September 15, 1968, just before my change of orders from sea duty aboard the *Davidson* to shore duty with the staff of Destroyer Flotilla Five in Pearl Harbor. In Navy terminology, individual ships are assigned to squadrons, which normally number eight ships, and a group of squadrons is then organized into a flotilla. The commander of Destroyer Flotilla Five in Pearl Harbor was a senior captain in charge of the overall readiness of all destroyers and destroyer-escorts in the Pacific. My staff job at the flotilla headquarters was to assist communications officers aboard ship in matters of readiness and training. It was just as I started this shore-duty assignment that I unwittingly opened a small door to the future.

The city of Honolulu was home to a Triple-A professional baseball team known as the Hawaii Islanders. They played in the Pacific Coast League (PCL) and enjoyed an exceptionally good season in 1968. All home games were broadcast live on local radio. However, since satellite communication was in its infancy and too cost prohibitive for commercial stations, the Islanders' road games, played in cities up and down the West Coast of the U.S. mainland, were broadcast using a method the legendary baseball broadcaster Red Barber and others had pioneered several decades earlier.

The announcer sat in a studio in Honolulu and received a ticker-tape shorthand version of the result of each pitch. For example, the letter "B" meant a ball, "Kc" was a called strike, "Ks" was a swinging strike, "F-7" stood for a fly ball out to left field, "2B-9" was a double to right field, and so forth. The announcer glanced at the tape and then made up the play-by-play based on what had happened, inserting sound effects to make it seem as if he were sitting in the broadcast booth right behind home plate.

I spent many late afternoons and evenings with a transistor radio ear-plug in my ear following the Islanders in their pursuit of the 1968 PCL title. During the Islanders' magical quest for their pennant, I began to envision myself doing what the guy at KGMB radio in Honolulu was doing, and I wanted to know more about it.

So, at the conclusion of the 1968 season, I called the radio station and asked the play-by-play announcer if I could come and speak to him about his craft. He graciously agreed. When we met, I realized that he was a young man, about a year my junior, and doing Islander games was his first full-time radio job. He gave me some ideas on how to practice doing play-by-play without actually

being on the air, thanked me for my service to the country, and
wished me luck.

Now, there are times when we may not remember the names
of the people we meet who help us along the way. However, in
this case, I will never forget that young Islander broadcaster who
was just starting his career. His name is Al Michaels, who today,
with credits such as Cincinnati Reds and San Francisco Giants
baseball, ABC's *Monday Night Football*, and the legendary U.S.
Hockey "Miracle-on-Ice" call against the Russians during the 1980
Olympics, stands as one of the most famous and widely acclaimed
sports broadcasters of all time. While I'm sure Al has little or no
recollection of our meeting, it was his encouragement and example
that helped me a couple of years later take the first step down a
similar career path.

My commitment to the Navy after graduation from OCS was
three years of active duty, but as the end of that period approached,
I had no idea what I would do for a living after the service. There
was no way to job hunt while stationed in Hawaii, so I decided to
extend my service time, get back to the mainland, and then figure
out my future. I applied for a nine-month billet at the Defense
Intelligence School (DIS), located in Washington, D.C. This
school trained junior officers from all four services - Army, Navy,
Marines, and Air Force - in the field of military intelligence. If
accepted, I would be obligated to an additional two years of service
upon graduation from DIS. The standard military practice was one
year of service owed for each six months or fraction thereof of
specialized schooling.

It was becoming more and more clear that my path began
to resemble my father's. Because he had spent his career in
intelligence, both in the Navy and as a civilian at the Pentagon, I
thought I would enjoy a similar challenge. I was accepted to DIS,
packed up the family, left Hawaii, and found a townhouse to rent in
suburban D.C. in time to begin classes in September, 1969.

The first two months at DIS were routine. Our class
numbered about ninety officers, and since the school calendar
was only nine months long, we were all asked before the end of

October to submit duty-station requests for assignments following graduation. This gave those in charge of duty assignments plenty of time to place each officer. We were asked to select three duty preferences and were told we'd get one of the three. I had become used to beautiful weather in Hawaii, so I requested the Naval intelligence offices in San Diego, San Francisco, and Pensacola, Florida, as my three choices.

About the middle of January, my classmates in the other services started to receive orders, and everyone was getting either his first or second choice of duty station. Three other Navy lieutenants and I became concerned when none of our orders were forthcoming. My orders finally arrived in mid-February, and I was told to report as a Naval intelligence liaison officer (NILO) in Vietnam. In other words, the Navy wanted me to crawl around rice paddies and gather intelligence about the movements of enemy Viet Cong units.

I was in total shock. First, the Navy did not live up to its promise, "You'll get one of the three duty stations you ask for." And second, I had made a lengthy deployment to Vietnam on the *USS Davidson* and had neither the interest nor physical ability to become an intelligence version of a Navy Seal. So, I spent a few days praying and weighing my options. Then I took action necessary to meet a specific deadline.

One week before the end of my first six months of DIS, I requested a meeting with the school's commanding officer and told him that I was withdrawing from the school, effective immediately. I don't think anyone had ever done this, so the CO didn't quite know how to react. He tried to talk me out of my decision, but I told him my mind was made up. The Navy could send me anywhere it wanted for one year, but not for two, because I had completed less than six months of schooling. I also figured that my chances of becoming a NILO in Vietnam would be slim, since each officer selected had to undergo six months of Vietnamese language training before deployment. I was betting the Navy would not invest six months of language training in me because I would be eligible for release from active duty just six months after the training.

And, as it turned out, I won what I felt may have been the biggest bet of my life. After a few weeks of sitting at home and hearing absolutely nothing, my detailer at the Bureau of Naval Personnel called me with fortuitous news regarding the operations officer at the U.S. Naval communication station in Asmara, Ethiopia. He was getting out of the service, and I would receive orders to leave immediately to replace him. I asked if my family could accompany me, and the detailer said yes, but not at military expense, since I only had one year of obligated service remaining.

In Navy terminology, "immediate-execute orders" normally mean you have 48 hours to report to your new duty station. However, in my case, this couldn't happen because I needed a passport and a series of shots related to travel in Ethiopia that could not be given all at once, so my orders were changed to "report as soon as possible." A quick sale of our car and other household items provided cash so that Rosemary and the children could make the trip with me. We obtained their passports and shots, and on Easter Sunday, 1970, Rosemary, Julie, Jeff and I flew halfway around the world to the town of Asmara, Ethiopia, located about 7600 feet above sea level in northeast Africa.

As it turned out, the volatile six-week juxtaposition from a student at DIS to an operations officer in a place where Ethiopian Emperor Haile Selassie came once a year to take advantage of American military dental work was all part of God's plan to facilitate my eventual broadcasting career, a career that I could never have known at the time would unfold in Lima, Ohio.

Sportscasting 101

A smara is a city in Eritrea, which in 1970 was an Ethiopian province, but, as I learned very quickly, it was also an area nine years into a fierce battle for independence from the motherland. Its roots go back hundreds of years. Until 1889, Asmara was little more than a small village when the Italians colonized it. For the next fifty years, thousands of Italians left Europe to build new businesses and industries in Asmara. The Italian influence in architecture and culture was so great that the city eventually took on the nickname *Piccola Roma*, which means "Little Rome."

When the British defeated the Italians in 1941, they colonized not only Eritrea but also the entire country of Ethiopia for the next ten years. The U.S. and British quickly negotiated an agreement for a U.S. military base to locate in Asmara because its altitude above sea level made it an ideal place for a communications link.

The Army opened Kagnew Station in Asmara in late 1941, and it became home to communication sites for several government agencies and all four armed services. The Navy component bore the name Naval Communication Station

(NAVCOMSTA), Asmara. Its mission was to relay radio teletype message traffic from any military or government agency to ships and other naval forces in the Eastern Mediterranean, the Western Indian Ocean and the Southern Middle East.

While advances in communication technology prompted the closing of Kagnew Station in 1977, when I arrived in 1970, it was a busy post that supported nearly two thousand military and civilian personnel and their families. The city population was less than 50,000, and Asmara had been in decline for nearly thirty years.

This decline happened for several reasons. First, even though they left an Italian administration in place in the 1940's, the British moved much of the industry and business from Asmara to the more developed British colonies of India and Kenya. Second, in 1952, the United Nations took control of the area from the British. The UN resolved to federate the former colony of Eritrea under Ethiopian rule and to move the country's capital city from Asmara some six hundred miles south to Addis Ababa. And third, in 1961, Ethiopian Emperor Haile Selassie added insult to injury by declaring the once-independent territory of Eritrea the fourteenth province of the Ethiopian Empire.

This was the last straw for the people of Eritrea. A group called the Eritrean Liberation Front (ELF) formed the same year and waged guerilla warfare for thirty years against the emperor and his successors before finally regaining independence in 1991. Although I don't recall any rebel fighting in Asmara while I was stationed there, the Ethiopian military did its best to eradicate the ELF in whatever manner possible. On several occasions, young men that I knew as waiters at the Officer's Club at Kagnew Station simply disappeared and never returned to their jobs. We never knew for sure, but the explanation heard most often was that government troops arrested them as ELF suspects and either put them in jail without trial or killed them.

Of course, Rosemary and I knew nothing about the political undertones in Asmara when we first arrived. We wanted our family to experience local culture as much as possible, so when we learned that we could rent a small Italian villa close to the base for the American equivalent of $50.00 per month, we declined base housing and took the villa. Additionally, we enrolled the children in an Italian Montessori pre-school, and also employed a young woman from a nearby village five days a week to clean, cook and occasionally watch the kids. Her salary of $25.00 per month was the highest amount allowed by Asmara authorities so as not to upset the local economy. That said, it represented a very good wage compared to other Ethiopian workers.

We were told by Kagnew Station authorities that we must hire a night guard if we lived off base. Night guards were elderly Ethiopian men who could no longer work regular jobs. We learned that the mere act of hiring a night guard was similar to paying mafia-like protection money. Having such a gentleman in our employ was a clearly understood signal in the community that our home was permanently off limits to any local Ethiopian considering property vandalism or theft.

Our night guard didn't actually guard a thing. He rode a bicycle from his village to our house once a week to wash the cars and mow the small patch of grass in the front yard. His monthly wage was $10.00, which, in that economy, was sufficient to support him. The night-guard system was Ethiopia's version of Social Security, and it worked like a charm. Elderly men had a means of support, and those who hired them had the fears of their homes being robbed assuaged.

Few military officers shipped cars to Kagnew Station at that time. The tradition was for an incoming officer to purchase his vehicle from the person he was replacing. So, when I arrived, I bought a seven-year-old Volkswagen bus for family use from my predecessor and also purchased a rusty-but-still-running 1936 Fiat from a local Italian for my short commute to and from the base. Asmara was home to many European mechanics that made a good living keeping cars imported from Italy years before in operation. My Fiat was 34 years old with two bare-metal floor pedals and a thread-bare interior, but its engine ran well and it was a perfect work car.

There were three chief petty officers on the NAVCOMSTA staff that ran the facility very smoothly. My daily routine as operations officer was to check the overnight message traffic, take any necessary action, update the commanding officer, and then turn things over to the duty chief and stay out of his way for the rest of the day. Frankly, it was an easy job with little stress, so I had time for other pursuits.

The most valued resource on base for most Americans was the Armed Forces Radio and Television Service (AFRTS). It was the only link to U.S. news, including news from the sports world, which was of great interest to me, and other than a small bowling alley and even smaller movie house, AFRTS was our sole source of entertainment. AFRTS had a limited staff of assigned military personnel but also welcomed volunteers to help broaden its programming options.

I stopped by the station shortly after arrival and told them I was interested in learning to do sports play-by-play. I said I had no experience but was an avid sports fan and felt I could do a passable job if given a chance. They had a staff air person who did radio news and read a few scores, so those in charge of programming decided to give me a chance.

Because communication was the sole focus of Kagnew Station, job sites were manned around the clock every day of the year. To help ease the daily monotony of military personnel standing relatively boring watches, the base had a well-organized intramural sports program complete with inter-service rivalries. It included leagues for flag football, basketball, and fast-pitch softball as well as individual competitions in bowling and badminton. Given my experience in college tennis, I entered the base badminton tournament and was lucky enough to take home the first-place trophy.

The first on-air sports broadcast of my life took place during the summer of 1970. The AFRTS engineers put a two-ton Army truck next to the sideline at the fifty-yard line of the base football field, ran a microphone cord a good city block back to the station, and gave me the assignment of describing a Saturday afternoon flag football game to base listeners.

I must have done a credible job because they asked me to do a fast-pitch softball game the next weekend. I did several more football and softball games over the next few months, and then it came time for the base basketball league to start.

Basketball was a big deal at Kagnew Station, and some site commanders thought they were NBA general managers. They worked the personnel system hard to get enlisted men with better-than-average athletic ability assigned to their commands. When I saw a 6'7" storekeeper with what I soon realized was college-level post-position talent report to the NAVCOMSTA, I knew my CO was serious about competing for the base title.

By this time the AFRTS station knew that I could deliver a good play-by-play broadcast, so it expanded its coverage, and I spent two or three nights a week during basketball season doing games from the post's gymnasium. The more games I did, the more comfortable I became, and I gradually developed a love for my spare-time hobby.

By the end of basketball season, I was nearly nine months into my one year of obligated service and faced with the identical scenario I encountered in Hawaii. I was thousands of miles from the U.S. mainland and still not sure what I would do after the service. Since I had an easy job, the family was thriving, the climate was like San Diego, and I was saving more than sixty percent of my salary each month because the cost of living was so low, I chose to extend my tour in Asmara for two more years.

Once that decision was made, I got more deeply involved at AFRTS. The broadcast schedule of softball, flag football and basketball games grew, and at the end of the 1971-72 basketball season, I was presented with an opportunity of a lifetime. One day, one of my chiefs came into my office and told me that if I wanted to broadcast a major basketball tournament over the entire European AFRTS network, he could make it happen. The tournament featured sixteen military teams from Southern Europe and Northern Africa, including our base champion club from the NAVCOMSTA. It would also mean doing fifteen games in five days in near 100-degree heat in Athens, Greece.

I had little thought of stress to my vocal cords or the extreme heat, and it took roughly a nanosecond for me to accept the offer. A few weeks later I found myself sitting in a jump seat inside a military cargo plane headed to Athens.

Announcing fifteen basketball games over five days by myself with absolutely no color man to help in carrying the broadcast in a steamy gym was a challenge, but I loved every minute of it. You might call it an epiphany because it was right then and there in that stifling gym well over five thousand miles from Lima, Ohio, that I made up my mind that I would pursue a career in sports broadcasting upon my release from military service.

Our time in Asmara left us with many fond memories. When we arrived in Ethiopia, Julie was three and Jeff, a toddler of eighteen months. For the next two and a half years, the children flourished in the Montessori school and, in short time, became bilingual in English and basic Italian. We learned much about the local culture and came to admire and respect the way of life of the Ethiopian people. While they were very poor and primitive compared to Americans, they were also very rich in character and love for each other.

For special recreation a couple of times a year, we drove three hours down the mountain, over a dirt road with more than two dozen hairpin turns to the seaport of Massawa and stayed at an Army R & R facility on the shore of the Red Sea. The local seafood restaurants were exceptional, and our time on the beach and in the water was very relaxing.

When I extended my tour in Asmara, my release date from active duty changed to June 30, 1973. However, by mid-1972, the Vietnam War was winding down, and one morning in September, a general message to all Navy commands from the Bureau of Naval Personnel arrived on my desk. The message listed the names of five hundred reserve officers who were to be released from active duty effective December 31, 1972. Lieutenant Michael J. Mullen, USNR, was on that list.

What followed was an exercise known as "taking advantage of the system." I now knew I was to be released early from active duty, a decision that was the Navy's, not mine. Since I decided initially before the news of an early release came to extend my duty, I did some research and found that this marked the first time in U.S. history that officers were being released from the Navy before their tours of duty expired. It had happened several times in the enlisted ranks but never in the officer corps. I wondered if, under these circumstances, the Navy offered some sort of severance pay.

So, I went to the man in charge of payroll at the NAVCOMSTA, who also happened to be an officer with a near-photographic memory. When I asked him if the Navy had any provision for compensating officers who were involuntarily released from active duty, he went to the Bureau of Naval Personnel (BUPERS) manual, which is roughly the size of the New York City telephone book.

Given his knowledge of that monstrous manual and his recall from using it, he found the one paragraph in the entire manual in less than two minutes that addressed this subject. I'm paraphrasing, but the paragraph said that any officer with more than six consecutive years of active duty who was involuntarily released from the service was entitled to, what the Navy called, "readjustment pay." The amount was two months' base pay times the number of years on active duty.

My officer commission date was December 16, 1966. My newly ordered release-from-active-duty date was December 31, 1972. This meant my consecutive time in service would calculate to six years and fifteen days. It also meant that the Navy, perhaps unwittingly, had to pay me a full year's salary in order to release me from active duty six months early. I couldn't help but be elated!

Because the early release of officers was unprecedented, I didn't want to take the chance of misinterpreting the BUPERS manual. I wanted a record of this unexpected windfall in writing. So, unbeknownst to anyone else on staff, I sent an official message from the NAVCOMSTA to BUPERS referencing the appropriate

paragraph in the manual, citing the official time in service for one
Lieutenant Michael J. Mullen, and requesting permission for the
command's payroll officer to issue Lieutenant Mullen readjustment
pay in the amount of twelve months' base salary upon release from
active duty. I received a message reply from BUPERS the next
day. It referenced my message and followed that with one word -
PERGRA - which is the standard military acronym for "permission
granted."

My accumulated unused leave allowed me physically to
depart Asmara in mid-December, although my official release
date from the Navy remained December 31, 1972. Before leaving
Africa, my family and I enjoyed a four-day photo safari in Nairobi,
Kenya. Our lodge was located near the base of Mount Kilimanjaro,
one of the most picturesque vistas in Africa. Even in December, it
was very warm in Kenya, so after checking into the lodge, we put
on our bathing suits and headed for the lodge's outdoor swimming
pool. Jeff, then just four years old but already an adept swimmer,
ran directly to the deep end, climbed onto the one-meter diving
board and did a cannonball into the water. There was no lifeguard
present, but two other adults were sitting in poolside chairs and
saw what happened. They sprang from their seats and were one
step from jumping in to rescue Jeff when they saw him surface
and easily swim the length of the pool. Our son was the talk of the
lodge that night.

Following our photo safari, we flew to Europe and spent
about ten days seeing sights in Rome and Florence, Italy;
Innsbruck, Austria; and Munich, Germany. Two separate incidents
reveal a marked contrast in how different countries in Europe
treated Americans in the early 70's.

After a few days of sightseeing in Rome, we rented a car and
drove to Florence. Upon our late-afternoon arrival, we secured
a room in an inexpensive boarding house, parked the car, and
then walked to a small local restaurant. The owner gave every
indication that he understood us when we ordered two full meals
and two extra plates for the children to share our food. When the
bill came, however, we were charged for four full meals. Naturally,

when we tried to have the amount due adjusted, the owner acted as if he didn't understand a word of English.

We grudgingly paid the bill. Later, things got even worse when there was no heat in our room that night and we nearly froze despite sleeping fully clothed with our winter coats on. The next day was Christmas Eve, and we couldn't wait to leave Italy and go to Austria.

The drive to Innsbruck was beautiful but tiring and took all day. Shortly before dark, we found a small family-owned hotel in the heart of the city, and what a difference we noticed from the moment we checked in.

The owner spoke fluent English and welcomed us with open arms. The hotel had a first-floor restaurant where we enjoyed a wonderful meal. While we were at dinner, our host took it upon himself to take the small Christmas tree from the front lobby and put it in our room just so our children could have a tree on Christmas morning.

After two more days in Innsbruck, which included a chairlift ride up to an alpine ski lodge where the kids made a snowman and watched the skiers go down the slopes, we checked out of the hotel. When I looked at my bill, I noticed there was no charge for our check-in night dinner. It was the owner's Christmas gift to an unknown American couple with two small children, one I will never forget.

Our final stop before heading home was Munich. During our stay, we enjoyed the city sights and ate Wiener schnitzel and drank mugs of German beer in the world-renowned Hofbrauhaus. Our lodging was a bed-and-breakfast where the woman of the house fawned over the children and fed us morning meals fit for royalty. The night before we were to fly home, I was able to tune in a nearby Armed Forces station on a bedside radio and listen to my Washington Redskins beat Dallas 26-3 in the NFC championship game, thereby earning a first-ever Super Bowl berth.

We returned to the United States the first week of January and headed for an unused apartment in Zanesville, Ohio, owned by Rosemary's grandmother. That apartment provided us temporary shelter while I focused on the next two items on my list. The first was to find as big a color TV set as possible so that I could watch my beloved Redskins take on the Miami Dolphins in Super Bowl VII on January 14, 1973. And, the second was to start driving around Ohio, with my resumes in hand, in hopes of landing a job in sports broadcasting.

Hello Lima

W hile I was able to build a small financial cushion during my Navy time in Ethiopia, I felt an urgency to find civilian work as quickly as possible upon our return to Ohio. I knew that having no experience in commercial radio would automatically exclude me from jobs in larger cities like Cleveland, Columbus or Cincinnati, so I concentrated my job search in smaller markets like Zanesville, Mansfield, Marion, Dayton, Lima and Toledo. I made visits to radio and television stations in all of these cities, spoke to as many general managers as would see me, dropped off my resume and tape of my AFRTS play-by-play, and then hoped for a chance to get my foot in the door of the broadcast industry.

After losing a few jobs to more qualified people or simply being told that there was no position available, an opportunity finally came in late March, 1973, when I met Mr. Charles "Chuck" Osburn, the general manager of WLIO-TV 35 in Lima. Chuck started at the former WIMA-TV in 1960 as a studio announcer. He quickly became a fixture in local television by hosting a half-hour afternoon kids' show from 1963 to 1965 and serving as co-host of the very popular Easter Straker show for fifteen years. Chuck

eventually earned the title of program director and was promoted
to general manager in 1970.

Chuck Osburn was an energetic leader and big supporter of
the Lima community, and our personalities clicked right away.
He gave me a short air-check to test my work in front of a studio
camera and then offered me a job as a weekend sports anchor and
news reporter.

Frequent on-air personnel turnover was then, and still is, a
fact of life in Lima television because, as one of the smallest TV
markets in the country, most new air-talent hires are beginners just
out of journalism school who work a year or two in Lima and then
move to a bigger market. I didn't study broadcast journalism, but I
did have experience with AFRTS, and I also offered, thanks to my
six years in the military, an on-air maturity that that was lacking
in others with whom I was competing for work. The job Chuck
was offering didn't include radio play-by-play, but since I needed
employment, it met the "foot-in-the-door" criteria, and I accepted
his offer.

The Mullens arrived in Lima from Zanesville in early April
of 1973 and moved into a rental property on East Eureka Street, a
couple of blocks south of Lima's town square. We chose that place
because the landlord, Lima attorney Alan Dobnicker, was willing
to forego a long-term lease and rent the unit on a month-to-month
basis. Thanks to my financial good fortune upon release from
active duty, we had money for a down payment on a house, but we
wanted to take our time and learn the area before committing to
such an important investment.

Our daughter, Julie, was ready to enter first grade, and son,
Jeff, was kindergarten age, so the plan was to find a home before
school started. With an intent to locate in the city and near the
television station, we eventually purchased the home at 1500 West
High Street, a two-story house with a basement on the northwest
corner of Woodlawn Avenue and West High Street. It was just
five blocks from my work and four blocks from the now-defunct
Roosevelt Elementary School on West Spring Street. We enrolled
the children for fall classes and settled in to enjoy our first taste of

life as civilian homeowners.

My hours at WLIO, an NBC network affiliate, were 3:00 PM to midnight, Wednesday through Sunday, with an hour break for dinner. I functioned as a news and sports reporter on the weekdays and then anchored the sports segment on the Saturday and Sunday night 6:00 PM and 11:00 PM local newscasts. Compared to today's electronic broadcast options, the equipment was primitive. Videotape hadn't emerged, so there were only two ways that reporters could produce local film footage for use on the nightly broadcasts.

The first way involved the use of a Super 8 home movie camera. The unit was small, light and easy to use, and it was one of the first cameras with the ability to produce color footage. Its downside included a grainy film quality, which made almost everything look a shade of either green or red, and its inability to record audio. So, for example, a reporter could take footage of a fire scene with this camera, but he could not record any simultaneous audio from those fighting the fire or witnessing the event. Super 8 film required at least four hours to develop, edit and prepare for broadcast once the reporter returned to the station. Since it didn't contain any audio, when the on-air talent used the film in a local telecast, he or she had to write the text to correspond to the footage on viewers' TV screens.

The second option for local film footage employed the use of a 16-millimeter camera. This was a large, heavy device that was mounted on a tri-pod during operation to ensure steady filming. The camera produced better quality footage than the Super 8, and it also had the ability to record simultaneous audio. Its downside was that it produced only black-and-white film, and it also required a photographer to accompany the reporter to set up and operate the camera.

Using this scenario as an example, when a reporter and a photographer covered a local fire scene with the 16-millimeter camera, the photographer took film footage from many angles, and the reporter could then plug a microphone into the camera and film an interview with the on-scene fire captain and, perhaps, a witness to the fire. However, the film took up to eight hours to develop, twice as long as Super 8, and then even more time to edit the footage and audio portions together into a complete on-air package.

Because of these limitations, it was virtually impossible to use same-day local film footage of any event that occurred after 4 PM. So what TV viewers in the 70's saw most often on the local evening news was footage of stories or athletic events that happened a day or two beforehand.

If I wanted to air an interview with a coach or athletic director, for example, I had to set the interview up a day or two in advance and schedule a 16-millimeter photographer to come with me to film the segment. So, my live weekend sports reports consisted of reading whatever up-to-the-minute scores were available, verbally highlighting other local and national sports stories, and occasionally showing an interview I had filmed earlier in the week.

Lima television legend Easter Straker was the most prominent personality on the WLIO staff in 1973. Her one-hour daily talk show, *Easter's Parade*, started in 1955 and was a fixture for nearly thirty years. She referred to her noontime show as "The Living Room of the Air," and over the years she interviewed many famous people including Eleanor Roosevelt, Hugh Downs and Phyllis Diller. The show had big ratings for a midday time slot and generated significant advertising revenue for the station because Easter did all commercials live during the telecast. Each fifteen-minute segment had a different sponsor, and Easter's ability to extemporaneously tout the advantages of local merchants led to long-term sponsor relationships and a waiting list of businesses eager to sign a contract for a rare opening on her show.

During one of her most popular segments, a young child was chosen to sit in the "Birthday Chair," a throne-like studio set with steps designed so that a child could climb into the chair, sit comfortably, and be able to talk face-to-face with Easter. Easter would converse with her young guests, give them lollipops, and then let them dip one hand into a jar full of pennies and keep as many as that hand could hold. Easter's final show on WLIO aired December 28, 1984. Her famous birthday chair and one of the first TV-35 studio color cameras from the early 70's are now prominently displayed on the main floor of the Allen County Museum in Lima.

Another popular TV personality from that era was Ric Bratton. He hosted a weekly half-hour talk show that aired Sunday evenings at 11:30 PM following the local news. Ric always had interesting guests, and on occasion, the station would send him to California or New York to film interviews with actors who appeared on popular NBC soap operas and prime-time television shows. And, it was one of Ric's Ohio guests in particular who left a lasting impression on me for a most unusual reason.

Ric was at the station one evening to film a future show with a woman from Toledo. I don't remember her name, but she had gained some notoriety as a psychic and had been widely interviewed by both print and electronic media. During a break in their work, I walked through the studio where Ric was filming the show, and he introduced me to his guest. We had never met, so she had no prior knowledge of me or my background. After exchanging some brief pleasantries, the woman looked at me straight in the eye and said, "You were a gladiator in a former life."

I, no doubt, appeared a bit startled, but I shrugged off the remark and went back to my office without giving it much thought. After arriving home, I relayed the story to Rosemary, and then, slowly, a strange sensation began to come over me. Now, I'm a person who normally doesn't remember what movie I saw two weeks ago, but the psychic's comment had stirred a memory from my childhood.

As a pre-teen in Silver Spring, I often attended the Saturday afternoon double-feature at our local movie theater with a couple of neighborhood pals. Admission price for kids was a quarter, and, for another quarter, we could purchase a big box of popcorn and soft drink. Of all those Saturday double-features, the only one I could recall was a showing of *The Robe* and *Demetrius and the Gladiator*.

Although I had never believed that humans experience multiple incarnations, when a psychic I'd never met told me within seconds of our introduction that I had been a gladiator in a former life, and, when someone who can't even remember recent movies he'd seen recalled from twenty years back two gladiator movies as if I'd just seen them yesterday, my outlook on reincarnation slowly changed from "I don't believe in it" to "Maybe there's something to this, but I'm still not sure." Perhaps, by chance, if I were a gladiator in a former life, it might explain my keen interest in describing athletic events.

By the summer of 1974, I had worked at WLIO for just over one year and was beginning to look for other broadcasting options. My passion was to do play-by-play, but the only opportunity I had for that at WLIO was a one-weekend local tennis tournament which the station broadcast from Lima's Westside Swim and Racquet Club.

In the late summer of 1974, a nearby radio station, WDOH in Delphos, contacted me and asked if I'd be interested in broadcasting high-school football games on Friday nights that fall. I went to my friend and boss, Chuck Osburn, to discuss this new opportunity. Knowing that my real passion was radio play-by-play and that I wasn't regularly scheduled to anchor the Friday night sports, he allowed me to adjust my work hours so that I could be available to freelance for the Delphos radio station.

My first assignment was a road contest featuring Delphos St. John's at Clyde, a school about 75 miles northeast of Lima in Sandusky County. The engineer at WDOH came to Lima, gave me the equipment I'd need, and showed me how to use it; but I was a rookie and didn't yet understand the normal protocol for such broadcasts. I made the mistake of presuming that the program director at WDOH had already contacted the athletic director at Clyde for permission to do the game, so I figured my only task was to gather information about both teams so that I'd be ready for the broadcast.

Now, since there were no fax machines in 1974, much less the Internet, items such as rosters, statistics, and general game-prep notes were difficult to acquire. Compounding broadcasters' preparation problems, many high-school coaches at that time loathed giving advanced details like starting lineups or season statistics to members of the media for fear that the information might wind up in opposing coaches' hands before game time.

On game day, brimming with more than my share of excitement to do something I discovered thousands of miles away and not far at all from the Red Sea a couple of years earlier, I drove to Clyde, anxious to do my first play-by-play work on a U.S. commercial radio station.

Upon arrival, I found the school's athletic director, told him the station I represented, and asked where I should set up my equipment in the press box. He looked at me as if I were crazy and said that no one from WDOH had requested permission to do the game.

Additionally, he also made it clear that Clyde High School did not permit live radio broadcasts of their home games. So, within five minutes of arriving at my first commercial play-by-play site, I faced the first of what would turn out to be many scenarios throughout my career that boiled down to listening to my own interior monologue that spoke the words, "Mike, do whatever you have to do, but get the game on the air."

My first attempt toward accomplishing that goal was to explain to the gentleman that WDOH's FM radio signal wasn't strong enough to reach Clyde, so his gate receipts could not be affected by local fans choosing to stay home and listen to the game on radio. He chose not to accept that Jesuit-inspired logic and continued to deny me permission to broadcast.

There was still about an hour until kickoff, and that left me time to explore one last idea. I found a pay telephone and called the control room at WDOH. I asked the board operator if the station had any kind of a tape-delay system. He said, yes, that he could record my audio onto a tape and then feed that tape through a machine that would delay the actual air broadcast by seven seconds. This was a standard fail-safe system used by any radio station with programming that included taking live phone calls on the air. Its purpose was to give the board operator seven seconds to flip a switch and turn off any unexpected inappropriate verbiage, including off-color language, used by a caller before it went over the airwaves.

Upon learning that the station had the proper equipment, I went back to the Clyde athletic director and politely asked him if he would consider permitting a "tape-delayed" broadcast of the game. He huddled briefly with the school principal and then grudgingly told me that, since I'd come all the way from Delphos, he'd permit me to broadcast the game only if I promised it would be on tape delay and not live. I gave him that technically correct assurance but also chose not to tell him that the broadcast would be delayed by only seven seconds. I felt secure, however, because I knew no one in Clyde could hear the station and uncover the full truth anyway. So, with the sports equivalent in mind of, "If a tree falls in the woods and no one is around to hear it," I proceeded with my very first broadcast for which I would be paid the vast sum of $20.00, one to which the good folks in Clyde would not be privy.

In a way, though, the athletic director unknowingly had the last laugh of the evening because when I asked him where I should sit in the press box, he said there was no room for media. The best he could do was give me a bleacher seat that was close enough for my telephone cord to reach the press-box phone jack. So, my very first football game on a commercial radio station was described from a wind-blown seat in the stands at the Clyde High School stadium with a briefcase as my lap desk and no way to secure the depth charts and stat sheets I had prepared. I'm sure the listeners in Delphos struggled as I did that night, listening to my account intermingling with gusts of wind and the staccato sound of my wind-blown papers, but their Blue Jays prevailed 12-9, lending credence to William Shakespeare's observation, "All's well that ends well."

A season of high-school football play-by-play, one filled both with challenges that needed to be surmounted but also the knowledge that the quality of the product was getting better, whetted my growing desire to move permanently from television to radio, and it also proved a harbinger of events destined to transpire for me. Later that fall, management at Lima's most popular radio station, WIMA-AM 1150, implemented an on-air format change that would not only become immensely popular but also affect the rest of my professional life.

Radio Calls

WIMA has the distinction of being Lima's oldest commercial radio station although it went through two transformations before ending up with these call letters. After debuting as WBLY in 1935 on AM frequency 1240, the call letters changed to WLOK in the early 40's. The station was owned by a 1920's Ohio State football legend, Lloyd Pixley, who was an offensive lineman and team captain. He played under John Wilce, who enjoyed a fifteen-year run as the Buckeyes' twelfth football coach. Mr. Pixley also owned Lima's WLOK-TV which operated on UHF channel 73.

Then, in 1955, two Lima businessmen spearheaded a major change in the Lima radio-and-television market. George "Bruff" Hamilton and Robert Mack owned Northwestern Ohio Broadcasting Company (NOBC), which had Federal Communication Commission (FCC) license rights to radio frequency 1150 AM and to television channel 35, but neither had yet been activated. Mr. Pixley passed away that year, and upon his death, NOBC purchased both the radio and TV assets of WLOK from his estate. The decision was then made to change both stations' call letters and frequencies.

After NOBC released the WLOK frequencies and call letters back to the FCC, it moved all programming to WIMA-AM 1150 and WIMA-TV 35. Three years later, the company acquired FM frequency 102.1 and, for more than the next decade, NOBC's three electronic media outlets operated under the same call letters and ownership, built large audiences, and became recognized as the broadcasting industry's leaders in Lima and the surrounding area.

The next significant changes to the Lima broadcast landscape came in 1970. The first was when the FCC granted WIMA-AM a license to broadcast twenty-four hours per day. Until that time, the station signed on at 6 AM and off at midnight. The second involved the arrival of a new general manager, Mr. Les C. Rau, who four years later would offer me my first full-time job in radio. As time evolved and I got to know Mr. Rau better, one fact became clear to me. He was quite simply one of the best in the business at his job.

The third and biggest change occurred in 1971 when the FCC ruled that, to better ensure journalistic fairness, television and radio stations in small markets could no longer be owned by the same company. So, Mr. Hamilton and Mr. Mack chose to keep the radio stations and sell the television side to the parent company of the *Toledo Blade* newspaper, and the call letters changed from WIMA-TV to WLIO-TV. The long-term result was that after more than a decade of co-existing as partners in the same company, the television and radio stations evolved into adversaries fighting for the same local advertising revenue.

As a way to get the most out of a limited budget and staff size, it was common in the early 70's for small-market radio operations with both an AM and FM signal to simulcast, which means to air identical programming on both frequencies. Radio in that era centered around a lineup of local personalities called disc jockeys. They played individual 45 RPM records or tracks from 78 RPM albums and blended in regular updates of news, weather and sports. WIMA featured a middle-of-the-road (MOR) music format designed to appeal to the broadest possible listener spectrum. The music was a blend of current Top-40 hits and old favorites, and between records, air talents such as Tom Francis, Joe Jansen, Bill Holden, Bob Nelson and others kept the audience engaged by talking about what was going on in the community and promoting upcoming events of interest.

From the mid-60's through the mid-90's, WIMA radio enjoyed what, in my opinion, was an extended version of its Golden Age. It was the medium through which area adults received their up-to-the-minute local news, weather and sports each morning. They either listened to the car radio while driving to work or listened at home while getting the kids ready for school. Television provided only national network morning shows with brief local-news inserts each half hour, and *The Lima News* was an afternoon newspaper, so radio dominated morning audiences. Until the arrival of the Internet and cell-phone technology, radio was the only place to find out if bad weather had affected schools and workplaces by forcing delays or cancellations. Local radio personalities were integral to the community, not only because of the information and entertainment they provided but also because they were involved in many civic organizations and projects.

In the spring of 1974, WIMA's general manager, Les Rau, made a bold decision that directly impacted my career path. He chose to stop airing MOR programming on both stations and to begin formatting a popular new national trend, country music, on the FM side. It was a savvy move by a veteran radio professional. Later that year, WIMA-FM changed its call letters to WIMT, was reborn as American Country T-102, became an overnight sensation, and today, 40 years later, still has the largest overall audience in the Lima market.

The man Mr. Rau put in charge of this new country-music format was Jack Stower. In the early 70's, Jack sold advertising and did some farm-news reporting and high-school play-by-play broadcasting for WIMA. And, as is generally the case with promotions, the tide that lifts one man's boat will lift another's, even if he's still working, as in my case, for the television competition across town. Stower's promotion to station manager of T-102 required him to give up his play-by-play duties, and that created just the opening I craved.

When I inquired about the sports position at WIMA, Mr. Rau was aware of my broadcasting abilities through my television work. He expressed an interest in hiring me, but his vision was for me to do sports for both radio and television. He believed that having one central sports figure in Lima would be good for all concerned and that the combined salary from both TV and radio would go a long way toward enticing a good sports talent to stay in the Lima market.

My boss at WLIO, Chuck Osburn, knew of my passion for radio play-by-play, and I didn't want to be surreptitious about my interest in the opening at WIMA, so I asked Mr. Rau to suggest his "shared-talent" idea to Mr. Osburn. I thought that if the two general managers saw merit in the plan, it would override the "us-against-them" attitude that began to grow three years earlier with the sale of the television station to out-of-town owners.

When Mr. Rau presented the concept to Mr. Osburn, it was met with little enthusiasm. Allowing me to do a few Friday night ballgames for a small FM station in Delphos was one thing, but the idea of permanently sharing a sports air-talent with WLIO's chief broadcast rivals in Lima was corporately out of the question, so Mr. Osburn said no to the idea.

Once Mr. Rau had his answer, a few days later he offered me the job as sports director at WIMA, but I had a tough decision to make because the base salary was less than the $4,200.00 per year I was earning at the television station. After talking it over with Rosemary and after securing an overall increase in income by negotiating an agreement that paid me a base salary of $3,600.00 as sports director plus $25.00 for every play-by-play broadcast, I decided to follow my dream, give my notice to WLIO, and take the job that would enable me to do play-by-play for high-school sports on a regular basis.

One of my first tasks as sports director was to find someone to work as my partner on the high-school basketball broadcasts that were just over the local horizon, and that's where a man destined to become an iconic figure in Lima broadcasting history became the catalyst that paired me with someone who would become not only my work mate but also one of the best friends with whom I would ever be blessed.

WIMA's popular morning air personality, Tom Francis, suggested I give John Barton a call. John was a Lima City Schools administrator who had experience as a junior-high basketball coach and had previously done some work as a color commentator for WIMA. I contacted John and asked if he'd be interested in working with me during the season. He said yes, and we embarked on a broadcast partnership that lasted the next quarter century.

The first game I broadcast for my new employer was the 1974-75 basketball season opener for Lima Senior High School. Little did I realize that, years later, the game's unusual details would put it into the same "memorably significant" category as my other two radio firsts - the truck-bed broadcast in Ethiopia and the tape-delay drama of my first broadcast over commercial radio in Clyde.

The date was Friday, November 22, 1974, and Coach Jim Romey and the Lima Senior Spartans faced a road test against Toledo Macomber, a vocational school located in the heart of the Glass City. When John and I arrived at the school, we noticed that the very small gymnasium was actually a converted swimming pool. Due to lack of funding for a new gymnasium, the Toledo school board at some point decided to fill in an indoor swimming pool at Macomber and cover it with a basketball floor. There was just enough space for a regulation-size court, but there was little sideline or baseline room, and the only place for fans to sit was in an area behind a mesh screen high above one sideline, a barrier that years before had prevented spectators from falling into the swimming pool.

The Macomber athletic director took us to our broadcast location, which was on the floor at midcourt opposite the team benches. There was a small table, two folding chairs, and one hundred feet of coiled phone cord with a jack on its end. When we sat down, our chair backs were against the concrete sidewall, and both front table legs were a full two inches inbounds. I said to myself, "We could get killed doing the game from these seats!"

Macomber's best player was sophomore guard Kelvin Ransey. He scored fourteen points that night and led the Macmen to a 67-56 win. After high school, Ransey signed to play for Eldon Miller at Ohio State, became an All-American and, following his time in Columbus, was a number-four overall pick in the NBA draft, playing six years in the pros.

Lima Senior was led by John McCullough, a 6'4" senior forward who led all scorers with twenty-one points. While John's star was just beginning to rise and so much more would evolve with the Lima boy who honed his skills while growing up playing against boys much older on the basketball courts on Haller Street and at the YMCA, suffice it to say here that he is the only athlete from Lima, Ohio, ever to play in the NBA. I have no idea how to calculate odds, but I wouldn't be surprised if I'm the only small-market high-school sports announcer in America whose first commercial radio basketball broadcast both emanated from a converted swimming pool and included not one but two future NBA players.

To extend those odds even more, the following Friday night's broadcast featured yet another future NBA star. Legendary coach Paul Walker brought his Middletown Middies to Lima on November 29, 1974. His starting lineup included 6'5" junior Clarence "Butch" Carter, and Butch and his talented teammates jumped all over Lima Senior, 79-53. Following his senior season, Carter was named Ohio's high-school player of the year. He signed with Bobby Knight and played four years at Indiana, scored more than 3,000 points in six years with four different NBA teams, and went on to become the head coach of the NBA's Toronto Raptors for two-plus years in the late 90's.

So, two games into my broadcast career at WIMA, I had, albeit unknowingly at the time, called two contests that included three future NBA players. A fourth high-school star would join that list a few weeks later but not before I experienced my first boys Lima Holiday Basketball Tournament.

This annual showdown featured Lima Senior, Lima Central

Catholic, Bath and Shawnee and was held in the Lima Senior gymnasium. It took place during the school break between Christmas and New Years and always drew sellout crowds. Two semifinal games were played one night and, twenty-four hours later, the losers met for third place and the winners, for the championship. The Spartans captured the 1974 Lima Holiday Tournament, but only by the slimmest of margins.

In the semifinal game, John Doxie and John McCullough combined for forty-two points, and Lima Senior thwarted a twenty-six point effort by Steve Mowery and edged Bob Fisher's LCC Thunderbirds, 68-66. The next night in the championship game, four Spartans scored in double figures in a 71-68 thriller over Bath. The Wildcats started five seniors that night, including cousins Mike Mauk and Greg Mauk. Mike recently left the area after a very successful football coaching career at Kenton High School so that he could watch his youngest son, Maty, play quarterback for the University of Missouri. Meanwhile, Greg has continued the legacy of Gretchen Prichard and enjoyed great success as head coach of the girls' basketball program at Bath.

By the mid-80's, Lima Senior's overall dominance of the Lima Holiday Tournament led to its demise when Bath and Shawnee decided to look for other schedule options. Those appeared quickly when Elida's new basketball coach, Chris Adams, crafted a similar event and invited Bath, Shawnee and LCC to take part in a season-opening tournament called the Elida Tip-Off Classic, a two-night basketball fest that still marks the beginning of the boys' varsity basketball season for these four local schools.

As for my wingman, John Barton, and me, while continuing to develop our own brand of on-air chemistry in our first season together in '74-75, the Spartans continued to work on their chemistry. Their next post-holiday encounter was a home game against Canton McKinley, a perennial high-school powerhouse from Northeast Ohio. The McKinley Bulldogs featured a player whose talents were coveted by every school in the Big Ten, as well as most other college basketball powers.

Phil Hubbard stood 6'7" tall and was built like an NFL tight end. He averaged twenty-two points and eleven rebounds a game, and when he showed up in Lima in early January, 1975, every Big Ten head coach or top assistant made Lima Senior's gymnasium their destination as well as many other college scouts.

The game turned out to be one of the best I ever saw in my thirty-one years of high-school broadcasting. Hubbard scored twenty points in the first half, but John McCullough tallied twenty-four as the Spartans trailed by just four, 37-33, at the break. Both coaches made defensive adjustments at halftime, so the two stars were each held to only one field goal in the third quarter. However, Lima's two guards, John Doxie and Steve Howard, contributed seven points apiece, and the Spartans took the lead 53-51 going into the final eight minutes.

Even though McCullough was a forward and Hubbard played center and they weren't guarding one another each time down the floor, they were indeed that evening's transcendent figures, carrying their teams down the stretch. Each scored ten fourth-quarter points, but it was the last of those combined twenty, two Hubbard free throws with three seconds left, that enabled Canton McKinley to edge Lima Senior 71-70.

John McCullough's stat line was eleven field goals and fourteen of sixteen at the free throw line for thirty-six points. Phil Hubbard made thirteen field goals and six of ten from the charity stripe for thirty-two points, and lots of college basketball coaches left the Spartans' gym that winter night very impressed.

The University of Michigan ultimately won the recruiting battle for Phil Hubbard, and following his All-American career in Ann Arbor, he played professionally for ten years and scored more than 7,200 points in the NBA.

As for John McCullough, in many ways, Hubbard's co-star that night, he would become more than just that other less-heralded boy growing up on Lima's north end who had the game of his life. As a matter of fact, John's chance to play in this game turned out to be a life-changing experience.

Indiana head coach Bobby Knight had assigned his top

assistant, Dave Bliss, to scout Hubbard against Lima Senior. Later that spring, Bliss left the Hoosiers to take the job as head coach at the University of Oklahoma, a school where basketball was pretty much an afterthought to Bud Wilkinson and his juggernaut Sooner football teams. As Bliss was putting together his 1975 recruiting plan, he remembered his visit to Lima and John McCullough's performance in that game that was supposed to be all about someone else.

It's important to understand that McCullough was a good high-school basketball player as well as an excellent student, but he was not at all on any Division One school's recruiting radar. John was what's known in sports as a "late bloomer." If Lima Senior had not scheduled Canton McKinley during John's senior year and if John hadn't played the game of his life against Phil Hubbard's team, his college-basketball options likely would have been, at most, choosing from amongst small schools such as Bluffton, Defiance, or Ohio Northern.

Oklahoma could not attract a player of Phil Hubbard's caliber in 1975, but something about John McCullough's performance remained fresh in Coach Bliss's mind. He likely pictured John as a good practice player, and maybe the seventh or eighth guy on his bench, but McCullough turned out to be much more.

Bliss ultimately offered the Spartans' best player a basketball scholarship, and John McCullough went to Norman and blossomed into one of the best players in Oklahoma history. As a senior, John averaged better than sixteen points per game, was named the Big Eight's player of the year, and led the Sooners to the NCAA Elite 8, where his team finally bowed out to Larry Bird and the Indiana State Sycamores, 93-72.

In the spring of 1979, John was the eighty-fifth pick in the NBA draft, a fourth-round selection of the Phoenix Suns. And, while he didn't make the Suns' roster that year, he did keep active in the semi-pro ranks, including a stint with Lima's own Ohio Mixers, and finally received an injury-replacement call-up from the Suns, one that lasted from early November to early December of 1981. He wore jersey number 8 for Phoenix, played sparingly in eight games, and scored a career total of 21 points. While to an NBA fan from somewhere else, John McCullough is no more than a professional basketball footnote, to fans in Lima, he remains the only local player to ever step onto an NBA court in a regular-season game.

Much later in my career, when I had the occasion to speak before groups of high-school athletes, I often used John McCullough's story to illustrate the importance of always giving one's best on the court or field because one never knows who will be watching. Dave Bliss was also watching John McCullough on the same night he was dispatched to Lima to watch Phil Hubbard in early 1975, and by giving his best, John wound up with a full scholarship to a major university and a basketball career that took him to a level no other Lima athlete has reached.

Lima Senior finished the 1974-75 regular season with a 12-6 record and then made a remarkable run in the post-season tournament. It started with a 49-44 sectional semifinal win over Celina and continued with a last-second victory over Findlay in the championship game.

There was no alternate-possession rule in high-school basketball at that time, so the officials would signal for a jump ball anytime two players had simultaneous possession. With about five seconds left and the game tied at 69, the referee called a jump ball at center court in the Elida Fieldhouse. The Spartans controlled the tip, and guard John Doxie tracked down the loose ball about 35 feet from the basket. He turned and let it fly just before the buzzer and drew nothing but net. The basket only counted for two because this was a decade before the three-point shot entered the rule book, but it didn't matter as the Lima Senior fans exploded onto the court and celebrated the 71-69 sectional championship victory over the Trojans.

The big-school Class AAA district tournament was played that year at Bowling Green State University's Anderson Arena. The Spartans dispatched Ashland 60-51 in the semifinal game behind John McCullough's twenty-four points, and John added twenty more two days later in the 62-52 championship win over

Galion. That set up a regional semifinal matchup against Columbus
Linden-McKinley at the Fairgrounds Coliseum in Columbus.

Linden-McKinley was led by veteran head coach Jene
Davis and featured sophomore Todd Penn, a lightning-quick point
guard who would later play at Ohio State. After three quarters,
the game was tied at 48, but despite a twenty-nine point effort by
John McCullough, young Mr. Penn made five clutch free throws
in the final ninety seconds, and his twenty-two points enabled the
Panthers to edge Lima Senior, 66-63.

The only solace for the Spartans was they lost to the eventual
1975 AAA state champions. Linden-McKinley beat Newark by
fourteen in the regional finals, Joe Petrocelli's Kettering Alter
team by two in the state semifinals, and then won the title, 77-72
over Cleveland Heights, the team that eliminated, of all schools,
Phil Hubbard's Canton McKinley by two points in the other state
semifinal game.

By April, 1975, I had a full season of basketball broadcasts
under my belt, and I knew that I had made the right career choice.
A mosaic of memories and anecdotes that transpired over the next
31 years at WIMA was about to begin presenting itself. It was a
mosaic comprised of memorable games and athletes and coaches,
one that also included a burgeoning friendship with John Barton
and others like George Frazee, who years later would join me as
a color analyst, and also a mosaic that showed the daily life of
a small-market radio sports director trying his best to present a
quality product in an age long before anyone would ever know
what it meant to Google information.

WIMA's Golden Age

While my radio career would ultimately include three different income-producing duties – department head, play-by-play announcer, and advertising salesman – my first few years at WIMA revolved around learning the many responsibilities of the sports director's job and polishing my descriptive skills on game nights. I quickly learned that sports programming was both an important and efficient income producer for the station. While it consumed approximately fifteen percent of the total annual air time available on WIMA, sports-related advertising produced more than thirty percent of the station's total revenue.

From its very beginning, WIMA's broadcast schedule included a full slate of local high-school sports, Ohio State football and basketball, the Cincinnati Reds and the Cincinnati Bengals. It was my job to see that those products were presented professionally and thoroughly to our listeners.

When I started at WIMA in late 1974, the studios were located on the top floor of a three-story building known as Gregg's Annex, which stood across the street from Gregg's Department Store in the 200 block of North Main Street in downtown Lima.

In addition to a few administrative offices, there was one studio for all live shows, another studio for production of commercials, and a newsroom with a small audio booth for airing live news and sportscasts during morning-drive time and for recording those to be used later in the day.

In the spring of 1977, the station moved to its current location just west of the former Lima YWCA at 667 West Market Street. This one-story building offered ample room for the existing operation, space for future growth, and much-needed parking for staff and visitors.

My typical weekday morning started with an alarm buzzer at 4:40 AM. I got up, brushed my teeth, threw on old clothes, and made the short drive to the station in time to arrive by 5 AM. This gave me just over an hour to prepare for my sportscasts, which ran twice each hour on both AM and FM between 6 AM and 9 AM. Each segment contained four minutes of information wrapped around a sixty-second commercial and was live for the first two hours and taped for the third hour. The reason for the taped third hour, I'll get to a little later.

While today's sports reporters have a limitless number of electronic information sources, during my first fifteen years at WIMA, the Associated Press (AP) teletype wire in our newsroom was the only place for me to obtain state or national sports news. After pouring a cup of straight black coffee, my first morning task was to gather the voluminous overnight accumulation of printed copy from the AP machine and separate the stories into piles of news, sports, weather, and farm-related information.

My stack included a three-to-four page summary of national sports news, a similar rundown of Ohio's pro and major college sports teams, a list of game scores from the current sport season, league standings for that sport, and an occasional feature story written by an AP staff writer. The only sources for local sports news were my own investigative work and information and scores phoned into the newsroom by area coaches.

Since our AP teletype machine operated twenty-four hours a day, it was naturally subject to an occasional breakdown, to a teletype ribbon that was too dry to produce legible copy, or to human error such as the evening news person leaving before making sure there was enough paper in the machine to last overnight. There were many times in my career when I had to make an emergency call to AP headquarters in Columbus about 5:15 AM and ask them to immediately retransmit some missing sports information in time for me to go on the air.

Once I gathered all of the material, I started to prepare for the morning shows. Preferring a conversational air sound, I never wrote out my sportscasts. I made notes on the AP wire copy and used a highlighter to mark sections I wanted to emphasize. There was no way to include all of the information in a four-minute broadcast, so my biggest challenge was to edit and organize based on my target listening audience.

Using Major League Baseball as an example, the vast majority of WIMA listeners were either Reds, Indians or Tigers fans, so I gave fairly detailed information on games involving those teams because this was the first chance for people with normal bedtimes to learn these results. For all other Major League games, I simply gave the list of winners in each league. Conversely, using hockey as an example, until the Columbus Blue Jackets began playing in the NHL, I never included a regular-season hockey score in my morning sportscasts and never received a single listener complaint. That told me that no one in my audience cared about professional hockey scores until it was time for the Stanley Cup finals.

My goal was to sound as if I were sitting across the table from the listener recapping the latest from the sports world. When I had a local story to report, I'd do my best to obtain audio from the person involved and use it on the air. Since WIMA's morning show host, Tom Francis, was also a big sports fan, we often talked about the latest sports news, especially during football and basketball season when the Ohio State Buckeyes were in the spotlight.

With regard to local sports coverage, one of the few complaints I routinely received from area listeners centered on the inclusion, or lack thereof, of results for high-school games in sports other than the fan favorites of football and basketball. Those sports had plenty of followers, and game scores were routinely reported to the station. However, the situation was quite the opposite for the so-called "minor" sports of volleyball, tennis, baseball and softball.

A few coaches, such as Elida High School's tennis coach, Denny Schwinnen, were faithful in calling results, but despite my annual plea to high-school athletic directors to urge their coaches to phone in scores, most never called or only did so after a victory. As a result, I had few "minor" sport scores to report each morning, and those I did have were almost always from the same schools. So, I would regularly be stopped in public and asked, "Why don't you ever announce our school's scores on the radio? You give ___'s scores all the time!"

Their tone usually suggested that I was deliberately playing favorites in my reporting by not mentioning their school's scores. I explained that the only reason I didn't give that information was because no one called in the results. That rarely satisfied them because, somehow in their minds, since I was the sports guy on radio, I should automatically know every result of every game, and, since I recognized early in my life that sports fans and rational thought often aren't the best of friends, no amount of explanation regarding my need for someone to call in the scores was going to change their opinion.

After a busy early morning, by the time 8 AM arrived, I was three cups of coffee into my workday but had not yet cleaned up or had breakfast. Since I lived only five minutes from the station, and since, for most of the year, my wife was at work and the kids were at school by this time, I taped my broadcasts for the 8 to 9 AM hour so that I could go home to eat, shower and shave without jockeying for bathroom space, and put on more appropriate work attire.

Upon returning to the station, I spent the rest of my day focusing on the myriad details of putting together broadcast schedules for high-school games, preparing for future game broadcasts, covering press conferences, doing investigative reporting on community sports stories, and updating and taping sportscasts for the noon and evening news blocks.

From the day I started at WIMA until the day I retired, I was given the greatest gift an employee can receive – the full trust of my employer to do the job. Les Rau was a general manager who went to great lengths to hire the best talent possible within the salary range available to a small-market radio station. He often boasted that WIMA's air-talent and overall staff could compete with any station in Cincinnati, Columbus or Cleveland, and I thought he was correct in that assumption.

While Les's forte was format programming and projecting a station's impact throughout the community, he was smart enough to let people do the job they were hired to do, especially in areas where he did not have personal knowledge or experience.

In my case, while Les was aware of sports and its importance to his company, he was not a big "fan." As a result, he never micromanaged my air work or questioned my decisions regarding local game broadcast schedules because he understood that I knew much more about sports than he did. I appreciated his trust very much, and it prompted me to work even harder to deliver a first-rate product that would continue to earn that trust.

One of my first goals as sports director was to impact and hopefully change the manner in which local game broadcasts were packaged and sold. During my first season behind the WIMA microphone, I learned that the sales staff sold game advertising based more on an appeal for community support than solid retail marketing. For example, the sales people took the roster of a local high-school basketball team, found out where each player's dad or mom worked, and then, where applicable, contacted those businesses and asked them to support the game broadcasts by buying two thirty-second commercials.

If I scheduled a tournament game featuring a school not normally on our airwaves, they would go through the yellow pages of businesses in that school's community and make last-minute phone calls hoping to attract sponsors. This procedure worked to a degree, but it was time-consuming and put considerable pressure on the sales staff. Additionally, there was always a question whether enough advertising could be sold for each game to cover production expenses.

After John Barton and I had a full year on the air together, I knew that our product was better than anything else in the market, so I suggested that we sell our high-school sports programming the same way network television did in that era. For example, if an advertiser sponsored ABC's *Wide World of Sports*, that advertiser didn't buy individual shows. Instead those who worked for that advertiser bought the concept of seeing different athletic events from around the world each weekend and the value of reaching viewers that they wished to target as potential customers.

I believed there was enough local interest in high-school sports for the same principle to apply. A balanced game schedule that proportionally showcased each of the Lima schools was, in my opinion, a worthy year-round advertising vehicle for any business looking to attract a sports audience and not just a donation in support of one's favorite high school.

Based on this theory, I convinced the sales manager to develop a package that gave a sponsor a "billboard" (name of their business) mention in the game open and close, plus two thirty-second commercials in any local sportscast aired on WIMA throughout the year. This covered regular season football and basketball games, all tournament contests in those sports, any spring-sport broadcasts such as a local high-school team playing in a regional or state baseball or softball tournament game, and, during the summer when the Reds had a night off, American Legion or Lima Locos baseball games.

The package offered a volume discount over individual game prices and when the sales staff started offering it to local advertisers, it became a big success. Our sales people sold enough advertising packages to not only cover expenses and produce a reasonable profit, but also leave a handful of sponsor availabilities so individual businesses that didn't have a year-long advertising budget but wanted to support their favorite teams were able to do so for a price they felt they could afford.

By the late 70's, the days of making frantic phone calls for game sponsors at the last minute were over. The sales staff could concentrate on other marketing efforts, and the sports department was able to deliver a top-quality local broadcast with a workable number of game commercials.

Since most breaks were sixty-seconds and none were longer than two minutes, advertisers' commercials received quality listener impact, and by being a part of every local game broadcast, each sponsor received the commercial frequency required to keep its business or service before the public throughout the year.

While my daily morning air work and responsibilities for the overall sports programming of the station were important tasks, to be honest, anyone with average radio talent and basic organizational skills could have done what I was doing.

However, I soon learned, when it came to play-by-play work, that a small-market sportscaster also had to fall somewhere between a jack-of-all-trades and good old Harry Houdini himself in order to successfully get on the air for a Friday night ballgame.

The Show Must Go On

Much of my fascination with pursuing a sports play-by-play career stemmed from the presumption that, once hired, all I would have to do was prepare information on each team, show up on game night, and have fun describing the action. That seemed to me to be the reality for people such as Marty Brennaman, the radio voice of the Cincinnati Reds for the past forty years.

Reality for a small-market high-school sportscaster was totally different than my perceptions of the duties of those far more widely known than I. For every one of the nearly 3000 games I did on WIMA, I was the scheduler, producer, director, transportation coordinator, chief on-site engineer, equipment carrier, roadie (as far as set-up and tear-down of equipment), telephone repairman, halftime-show guest finder, statistician, and, oh yes, play-by-play announcer. Let's just say it was difficult to be as relaxed at game time as my listeners, whose only pre-game challenge was to open a cold beverage, proceed to their favorite recliner, and turn on the radio.

From a technical standpoint, what people actually hear when they turn on a radio is the result of a fairly simple two-step

process. In step one, audio (either voice or music) is sent by wire
from a station's broadcast studio to the site of its transmitter and
transmitting antenna. In step two, the station's transmitter takes
that audio and sends it out over the airwaves at various levels
of licensed power enabling it to be picked up by specially tuned
receiving units called radios. For example, WIMA in Lima is
licensed to broadcast at 1000 watts, which gives it a daytime
range of 75-100 miles. In contrast, WLW in Cincinnati broadcasts
at 50,000 watts which means it can be heard throughout Ohio,
Indiana and Kentucky.

All that's needed to deliver audio information to a radio
listener from a location outside a broadcast studio is to establish a
means of transmission from the remote location back to the studio
and then repeat steps one and two above. My standard answer
when asked how I broadcast games from distant cities was, "If
I can find a dial tone, I can get on the air from anywhere in the
world."

One of my sports-director duties was to ensure that there was
a reliable method in place to deliver the play-by-play account of
scheduled ballgames back to the WIMA studio. For most of my
career, I had only two options. Either I needed a working telephone
line in place in the press box, or I needed to take a Mobile Area
Radio Transmitting Instrument (MARTI) with me for use at the
game site.

The MARTI is a miniature version of a larger station
transmitter. It's the size of two briefcases stacked on top of each
other. When attached by a cable to a portable or pre-positioned
permanent antenna, and after a microphone is plugged in, the
announcer can send an audio signal back to a receiving antenna at
the radio station and thereby get on the air.

I used the MARTI for most local sports broadcasts because
the stadiums and gyms were close enough for its signal to reach the
receiving antenna at WIMA and because it was much cheaper than
having phone lines installed at every location. To make matters
easier, the station engineer mounted permanent antennas at all
local football stadiums and also in local gyms where the MARTI

electronic signal was strong enough to get out of the building and back to my home station. He also left enough antenna cable to reach the press box or gym broadcast location.

To broadcast a local football game, for example, all I had to do upon arrival at the stadium was attach the antenna cable to my MARTI, plug in headset microphones for my partner John Barton and me, turn on the machine, and we were ready to go on the air. The process was equally routine at most gyms, with one exception, and that was Shawnee High School in Lima.

The only place to mount a permanent antenna in Shawnee's Lappin Gymnasium was in the rafters above the floor. In order to attach the antenna cable to my MARTI at Shawnee, I had to walk to the top of the home-side seating area, climb a permanent iron wall-ladder to a catwalk, imitate one of the Flying Wallendas about fifty feet out into the rafters, locate the coil of extra antenna cable, and then slowly drop the cable to the courtside broadcast location. When the game was over, I had to repeat the climbing process and recoil the cable onto the catwalk to get it out of the way until the next broadcast at Shawnee.

From an engineering perspective, MARTI games were by far the least stressful because the failure rate of the equipment was extremely low. And, since all MARTI games were within range of the station, I could monitor the air signal of my own broadcast using a portable radio earplug underneath my headset microphone.

Broadcasting road games beyond the reach of a MARTI signal posed a much more difficult challenge. While technology would eventually produce a portable unit that combined the functions of a telephone, an amplifier, and even a computer data link, the first twenty years of my career required a far more primitive setup.

During that time, I had to order the installation of a regular telephone line at each out-of-town game site. The line had to have an assigned number and a standard jack that I could plug into and get a dial tone. I also had to order a voice coupler. This was a device that functioned as a regular telephone but also had the capability of being connected to an amplifier that contained

two audio input channels. Once I dialed the station on the voice
coupler, the amplifier then enabled John and me to use separate
headset microphones, provide a better quality audio signal, and
keep both hands free to keep stats and organize depth charts during
the game.

Despite my best efforts to ensure and verify the installation of
an away-game phone line, there were several times during the early
years when the failure to install the equipment I ordered required
me to revert to my mantra from my very first broadcast night in
Clyde, "Mike, do whatever you have to do, but get the game on the
air."

The first major technical problem I recall occurred during the
first boys' state basketball tournament that I broadcast in March,
1975, from St. John Arena on the campus of Ohio State University
in Columbus. At that time, the university operated its own private
telephone system from within St. John Arena. Instead of ordering
a broadcast phone line from a company like Sprint or United
Telephone, I had to order a line from OSU's athletic department for
the state tournament.

When John Barton and I arrived at St. John Arena that year
for the first two semifinal games, an engineer at courtside assigned
specifically for the state tournament checked our line and made
sure everything was in working order. All went smoothly for
the Thursday and Friday semifinal games, but on championship
Saturday, less than an hour before the late-morning start of
the Class "A" finals between Marion Local High School and
Gnadenhutten Indian Valley South, our phone line went dead.

Naturally, I summoned the tournament engineer as quickly
as possible, but he could not immediately solve the problem and
had no other line available in his system for us to use because they
were all assigned to other radio stations. My only chance to get
the game on the air was to ask a big favor of a friend and fellow
sportscaster, Mick Acheson, who was working for WKTN radio in
Kenton, Ohio.

This was an important broadcast for WIMA because
Marion Local is located in Maria Stein, Ohio, a small village

approximately forty miles south of Lima, and coach Irv Besecker's Flyers were the only area team left with a chance to win a state title that year. While all but a handful of people from Maria Stein were in Columbus rooting on the Flyers in person that morning, our 1150 AM signal was a primary source for the thousands of other basketball fans throughout Northwest Ohio to hear the game back in a time when the state finals were not televised live on the air as they are now.

I explained my phone-line dilemma to Mick and asked if WKTN would mind relaying their audio to the WIMA studio so my station could carry the game as well. He not only quickly agreed but also graciously asked me to join him on the broadcast so the WIMA listeners would be able to hear a familiar voice throughout the game.

I called my station and explained the situation. The WIMA board operator then placed a phone call to WKTN to get their audio feed and about two hours later, Mick and I finished describing Marion Local's first state basketball championship win, a 59-56 overtime thriller over coach Charlie Huggins and the Indian Valley South Rebels, who were making their fourth straight state tournament appearance. While John Barton got an unexpected game off, I did play-by-play for the first and third quarters and Mick called the action during the second and fourth quarters.

My mission to get the game on the air was accomplished, and I've never forgotten the generosity of Mick Acheson and WKTN in making that possible. Although this incident occurred during my first basketball season in radio, I observed through the years that, despite some inherent competition for listeners, it was standard practice for broadcasters to help each other out at game sites in times of equipment malfunction. We all carried spare equipment, and we had each other's backs when it came to getting a game on the air.

As a postscript, if the name Charlie Huggins sounds familiar, it's because during twenty years of coaching at six different Southeastern Ohio high schools, his teams won 398 and lost only 74. He won three state titles, including two at Indian Valley South, and he was elected to the Ohio High School Basketball Coaches' Association Hall of Fame in 1993.

His son, Bobby Huggins, was a senior on the 1972 Indian Valley South state championship team. After a standout playing career at West Virginia University, Bobby later became the head basketball coach at the University of Cincinnati and currently fills the same position at his college alma mater.

While I have at least a dozen career memories of needing to find unusual, last-minute ways of getting a game on the air, the closest I came to failing that challenge occurred in the fall of 1978, and it involved a road football game for Lima Central Catholic. Needing to fill a one-year opening in their '78 schedule, the Thunderbirds found a school they had never played before with a similar one-time-only contract need. I'm not sure why the game was scheduled on a Saturday night instead of in the normal Friday night time slot, but LCC agreed to play Patrick Henry High School in the rural Henry county village of Hamler, about sixty miles north of Lima.

Since the school's football field was literally carved out of a cornfield at the intersection of two country roads, I knew it would require a special effort to make sure a phone line was in place for the broadcast. After learning that Hamler was served by a small locally owned telephone company, I contacted them several weeks before the game and ordered both a dial-up telephone line and a voice coupler.

I made sure the order taker understood that it was a Saturday night game. I also asked that the installation take place the day before the contest and that the installer personally call me at WIMA from the Patrick Henry press box to verify that the telephone line and voice coupler were in place and operational.

Shortly before noon on the Friday before the game, I received the phone call I had requested, and the installation man assured me that he was standing in the Patrick Henry press box and talking to me over the voice coupler. I felt confident that if anything went wrong the following night in Hamler, it would have nothing to do with the phone line or equipment. Boy, did I turn out to be wrong!

Because unexpected problems were a fact of life when doing a remote broadcast, whenever John and I traveled to a new venue, we made it a point to get there about two hours before game time. We arrived at the Patrick Henry football stadium shortly after six that evening for an 8 PM kickoff. My first clue that it might be a long night came as we walked up through the stands toward an old, weather-worn press box that looked as if it might blow over in the next cool early fall breeze. Upon entering the small enclosure, I immediately searched for my phone jack and voice coupler, but they were nowhere to be found.

Keep in mind this was the late 70's. That meant cell phones did not yet exist, and I was in a football stadium in the middle of farm country with no working telephone available. The main school building was within sight down the road, but there was no one there on a Saturday evening. Given these circumstances, I did not like my chances of getting this game on the air, but I had to exhaust every possible option.

My good friend and broadcast partner John Barton was a very laid-back guy who would have been just as happy to skip the game and spend the evening drinking a few beers at the nearest Hamler watering hole, so, while he walked back to the car to enjoy one of his regular cigarette breaks, I headed for a cinderblock structure beyond the corner of one end zone. I surmised that it was the Patrick Henry team locker room and hoped that it had a working telephone.

Upon entering the locker room, I saw an office cubicle in one corner that belonged to the head coach, but there was no one in the office and no sign of a telephone on the desk. I asked a couple of players who were just starting to dress for the game if the coach was available. They said no, but they did manage to locate the building custodian for me.

When I asked the custodian if there was a phone I could use, he told me that there was, but it was *on top* of the coach's cubicle and not *in* the office (I couldn't make this stuff up, folks!). He then explained that on weekends, the coach hid his phone *on top* of his office, hopefully to stop what apparently had been a recent rash of unauthorized long-distance calls made by student pranksters using the locker room phone.

After explaining the need for a quick fix to my press-box dilemma, the custodian found a stepladder, and from a perch three rungs up that ladder, I was able to reach the coach's phone. In the late 70's, small local telephone companies still employed people as information operators. And sure enough, when I dialed zero, Millie, a friendly-but-mature female, came on the line and asked how she could help me.

I told Millie about not finding either a phone jack or a voice coupler in the stadium press box after being told the day before by their company installer that he was standing in the press box speaking to me over that very equipment. Her response was something like, "Oh, you're talking about Fred."

After politely but firmly ensuring that Millie was aware that I needed Fred's services within the hour in order to broadcast the game, she told me that he was at the church picnic that evening and, although she couldn't promise, she would do what she could to contact him and have him come to the stadium.

I thanked God for phone operators like the small-town friendly Millie, who knew everybody in town and the best way quickly to track them down, and then went back to the press box. After explaining my progress to John, he and I got everything ready to go, just in case Fred showed up in time. And, just when all appeared to be lost and John could almost taste that first beer, sure enough, about fifteen minutes before kickoff, a gentleman in a telephone company jacket with a box under his arm started to jog up the bleacher steps toward the press box. Moments later, Fred was re-installing the phone jack and putting the voice coupler in place. He finished four minutes before kickoff.

I was doing my best to lower my blood pressure so that the radio audience wouldn't suspect what I'd been through for the previous two hours. Before I dialed WIMA to go on the air, I looked at Fred and said in an exasperated tone, "Why the hell did I have to go through this? I just talked to you yesterday in this press box, and you said everything was set to go!"

Fred obviously had never looked at the Saturday "date of service" on the installation order because his response was, "Hell, football games are played on Friday nights! I came back this morning and took out the equipment because we only have one of these voice couplers, and I didn't want anyone ripping it off over the weekend." So much for good client-vendor communication!

When I added up the effects of the emotional roller coaster of the pre-game saga, a game broadcast hampered by a first-half rain that smeared all of my depth charts and stat sheets because the ancient press box had no windows, and an eventual 15-13 LCC loss, I made myself a quiet promise never to schedule another broadcast from the football home of the Patrick Henry Patriots. Fortunately, I never had to test that self-promise, because no local team ever played football at Patrick Henry again during the rest of my career.

A decade after I walked down that Hamler "phone line-foul up" lane, John and I found ourselves in Middletown in the most unique physical broadcast location of my entire career. It was the 1988 football season, and Lima Senior had a Greater Miami Conference road game scheduled against their oldest and fiercest sports rivals, the Middletown Middies.

John and I had done games from Barnitz Stadium in Middletown on several previous occasions, so I was familiar with the broadcast setup. Unlike my experience ten years earlier in Hamler, ordering a phone line for a Middletown game was routine. A permanent telephone jack was present in the visiting team broadcast booth, so all I had to do was call the major phone company in Middletown and place an order for the visitor's broadcast line to be activated on the date of the game. WIMA had also purchased its own voice coupler by that time, so no extra equipment was needed.

On game day, John and I made the 100-mile trek down I-75, grabbed a bite to eat in Middletown, and proceeded to the stadium. Our good friend and Middletown High School athletic director, Ed "Skeeter" Payne, greeted us and said to let him know if we needed any help. He didn't even bother to take us to the press box because we'd been there before and knew where to go.

I hooked up the broadcast equipment to the phone line in the visitor's broadcast booth but cringed when I didn't hear a dial tone. I would find out days later that another communication glitch within the phone company had caused the problem, but, since there was no equivalent of Millie in Middletown in the late 80's, suffice it to say that it was impossible on a Friday night to summon a union telephone repairman in the time available to remedy the situation.

With the visitor's broadcast booth now out as an option, and no other phone line available in the press box, I hunted down Skeeter and asked him for the location of the closest live stadium phone line outside the press box. He said it was in the maintenance office below the home-side stands.

I always carried about 200 feet of extra telephone cord in my car trunk for those "just-in-case" moments when a backup plan had to be enacted. So, I got the line from the car, went to the maintenance office, plugged one end into the phone jack next to the desk and ran the cord as far as it would reach. After coming out of the office and up through the fan-access ramp to the stands, my phone cord reached as far as the fourth row of the bleachers at about the twenty-yard line.

You know my mantra by now, so John and I spent the next three hours sitting on concrete bleacher seats barely above field level, doing our best to describe a football game we could hardly see once the teams reached the other side of mid-field. We also had to contend with a steady stream of kids running by and distracting us with giggles and observations such as, "Look, these guys are on the radio! What are they doing in the stands?"

Just as the Lord had provided Millie to save the night for me in Hamler, my guardian angel in Middletown ten years later turned out to be an articulate and energetic public-address announcer. Whenever the teams were beyond my sight line and depth perception at the far end of the field, I slid one earpiece from my headset off my ear and listened carefully to the PA man describe the play.

For example, he'd say, "Jones on the carry, gain of four, second and six, Middies at the 22." I'd then say over the air, "Smith hands to Jones. He goes off left tackle about four yards before being stopped by the right side of the Spartan defense. It'll be second and six Middletown at the Lima Senior 22-yard line." I don't think many listeners back home had any idea I was describing action fifteen to twenty seconds after it actually took place.

Thanks to Middletown's excellent PA announcer and to a relatively mild and wind-free night in late September, John and I made it through the entire broadcast from those uncomfortable bleacher seats. It was worth the effort because Lima Senior played extremely well and beat Middletown 21-3. The 1988 Spartans would go on to an 8-2 regular season and become the first team in Coach Leonard Rush's time at Lima Senior to make the playoffs.

While engineering and phone-line issues were constant challenges in small-market sports broadcasting, the most frequent question I've been asked about my career is, "How did you keep all those names straight when you did a game?"

Play-by-Play Anatomy

When I reflect on nearly forty years of describing athletic events to listeners who, in all but a few circumstances, can't see what I'm seeing, the greatest compliment I could possibly receive can be summed up in a seven-word sentence, "I thought I was at the game." I'm thankful to say that I have been blessed with many such compliments throughout my career.

While it was common at local area games for a few diehard fans to sit in the stadium or gym and listen on a transistor radio to the WIMA broadcast of the very contest they were watching, the vast majority of game listeners were at home, in their cars, or at work. My challenge was to describe the total game experience in such a detailed word picture that listeners could enjoy the action as if they were watching it in person.

In order to achieve this result, I relied on a variety of tools and techniques, some of which I seemed to have a natural inclination to do well while others were the product of hard work and practice. While my Creator gets credit for my strong radio-friendly voice, my passion for describing athletic events, and a natural proclivity for organization and detail, whatever measure

of success I achieved as a play-by-play broadcaster was directly
related to the time and effort devoted to game preparation.

When fans asked how I so easily kept up with the action and
player names, I had difficulty answering because the formula for
a smooth broadcast was so complex. The ingredients included my
aforementioned fortes, specific score sheets I designed for myself
to make sure all needed data was at my fingertips, and appropriate
pre-game study. Of equal importance to broadcast quality was
building a descriptive ebb and flow so that a great play in the first
quarter didn't carry the same urgency or emphasis as a great play
with thirty seconds left in a tie game. I also had to learn to repress
the instinct to shout over a noisy crowd and to simply let the
microphone absorb a measured vocal input and do the job it was
built to do.

For football I designed offensive and defensive depth charts
which, after being filled in by position with complete data on
starters and backups, were placed back-to-back inside an 8 1/2" x
11" clear plastic cover. With one simple flip of each team's depth
chart after a change of possession, I was ready for the next play.
After determining what information I wanted and needed during
a broadcast, I created two separate single-page scoring sheets
which enabled me to recap the action at any point in the game. On
one sheet I logged each play with yards gained and whether the
play resulted in a first down. The other sheet contained all scoring
drives in order of occurrence, and I used different colored ink pens
for each score each team made for easy visual reference.

For spotting purposes during a football game, I made sure
I had numerical rosters for each team taped to an area within
easy eyesight. One of my career pet peeves centered on a handful
of athletic secretaries who sent me their football rosters in
alphabetical rather than numerical order. If you think about it,
of what use is such a document for anyone at a football game,
much less a radio broadcaster? If a fan in the stands sees number
37 make a great tackle and wants to find out who the player is,
a program roster in alphabetical order is of little help. He has
to search through the entire roster until the number 37 appears

before a name and is likely to miss at least the next play doing so. Therefore, any time I received an alphabetical football roster, I had to retype it myself in numerical order so that it could fulfill its intended purpose.

Another indispensable aid I happened upon for football broadcasts was a round two-piece yardage calculator about the size of a salad plate, which was one of a handful of items given to me by Jack Stower when I took over his WIMA play-by-play duties. The circumference of the bottom piece contained hash marks for each yard of the 100-yard field. The five-yard increment lines were a bit longer than the one-yard lines, and the ten-yard increment lines were even longer.

The top piece was smaller and attached to the bottom piece by a metal grommet so that it could easily rotate. It too had yardage lines around its circumference, but its purpose was to give instant total-yardage amounts at the end of a play. For example, if the ball was on a team's own 23-yard line, I would place the starting arrow on the smaller calculator piece at the 23-yard line of the larger piece to indicate the line of scrimmage. Let's say the next play was a completed pass that went all the way to the opposing team's 29-yard line. By simply finding the yard line where the play ended on the larger piece and glancing down, I could instantly see that the play covered 48 yards by the information on the circumference of the smaller piece.

That unique calculator, which worked equally well for both positive and negative yardage plays, made me sound like a math wizard during every football broadcast. After more than twenty-five years of repeated hand and finger contact made the device worn and almost unreadable, I made a call to the out-of-state distribution company printed on the back to purchase a replacement, only to find it had long ago gone out of business. An extensive search for a similar broadcast aid proved fruitless, so I gingerly protected the original for the remainder of my career.

While a basketball game was a quicker and more challenging audio picture to paint, it was also a more broadcaster-friendly sport because the rosters were considerably smaller than football and I could distinguish players by facial recognition and not just by a distant jersey number below a faceless helmet. As I did for football, I designed my own basketball score sheet with room for both teams on one legal-sized piece of paper. Those sheets provided more room than a typical basketball scorebook so I could annotate all the stats I wanted for each player. The starting lineup consumed the first five lines for each team, and I then listed the rest of the players in numerical order for easy substitute reference. I differentiated statistical information by a variety of pen colors and kept score with pencil so I could easily correct any errors.

During basketball season I also kept a three-ring binder with result sheets for all area teams. I would spend a couple of hours each weekend transcribing box scores from *The Lima News* so that I had running scoring totals not only for the teams on the WIMA broadcast schedule but also for the players on those teams. In the era before computers and e-mail, this was the only way I could provide listeners with information like scoring averages and season-high individual-game accomplishments.

My reason for going into such detail about game preparation is to explain why it's so difficult to answer the question that you, as a fan, may have asked, which is, "How do you do what you do?" In a nutshell, my end product was the combination of the abilities I discovered I had, hard work, and a few tricks of the trade picked up over time. When I think about what it took for me to bring my listeners a quality game-broadcast product, I'm reminded of a story that shows the limitations that often make successful outcomes unlikely if not impossible.

There was a time long ago when the sink faucet in our master bathroom was leaking and needed to be replaced. I figured that an intelligent 40-year-old guy should be able to replace a simple sink faucet without too much trouble, so I purchased a replacement faucet and set about the task one Saturday morning. After approximately three hours of sweating while on my back in a cabinet opening way too small for my arms and upper body, trying to make basic household tools do a job they weren't meant to do and finally stripping the threads on the new faucet pipes, I came to a conclusion I've remembered ever since, which is that it took me until I was 40 to figure out why God made carpenters and plumbers! I dialed the closest plumber to come and install a new faucet and never again tried to take on a task that I had neither the talent nor the proper tools to accomplish.

I recount this story because over the years I've heard a few high-school play-by-play announcers who very much resembled me trying to change that sink faucet. They had neither the talent nor the proper tools to accomplish their tasks. An experienced plumber with the right tools can change a sink faucet in ten minutes. Similarly, an experienced play-by-play announcer with the right tools can make a game broadcast sound as if a listener is sitting there in person.

However, I certainly wasn't the only one who was responsible for the finished product I helped author. In my case, I was so very blessed in my career by having men, three in particular, who possessed both the passion and the talent to help me do my job well.

Simply put, it sure does help to have the right sidekicks.

My Three Amigos

While I was extremely fortunate to have game-broadcast partners like John Barton and George Frazee throughout my three decades at WIMA, I could never have succeeded at my job trifecta of sports director, play-by-play man, and advertising salesman without the counsel and friendship of perhaps the most iconic figure in Lima radio history, Tom Francis.

Neither Tom nor I grew up in Lima, but both of us came to this city for job opportunities after our military service, and we both chose to make Lima our permanent home. Tom Francis was born in Columbus, Ohio, in August, 1934. Upon graduation from Columbus North High School, he went to college right next door at Ohio State University and graduated in December, 1956, with a degree in radio speech.

Tom enlisted in the Army in early 1957 and married his college sweetheart, Jean Corcoran, in June of that year. They spent the first of their 56 years together in Poitiers, France, where Tom worked as a public-information specialist. His job was to interview other American servicemen throughout France for articles which were then sent back to the USA for publication in their hometown newspapers.

Upon completion of his two-year enlistment, Tom accepted his first civilian job with WIMA radio in February, 1959. He often told me that he and Jean never expected to be in Lima more than a year or two, but as so often happens in life, his first job turned into an entire career, and he spent the next fifty years enriching the lives of thousands of people in Northwest Ohio with his engaging on-air personality; his unswerving and positive support of the Lima community; and his devotion to his family, church, Optimist service club and his unflagging allegiance to his beloved Ohio State.

By the time I started doing morning sports reports for WIMA in late 1974, Tom was already more than a decade into his position as the number-one radio personality in Lima. He anchored a group known as "The Big 'T' Team" in the mornings, which included newsman, Neil Winget; myself on sports; and live, over-the-phone weather forecasts from Gil Gomez and his staff, who were part of a Pennsylvania company known as Accu-Weather.

Tom Francis was bright, cheerful, professional, and always a perfect gentleman. Since we both enjoyed racquet sports, we spent many leisure hours together as friendly opponents playing tennis on Tom's Sherwood Park neighborhood courts or racquetball at the Lima YMCA.

As our friendship grew, Tom gradually took on the role of the older brother I never had. He wisely advised me to partner with John Barton on ballgame broadcasts and showed me the importance of giving the audience a complete update of news, weather and sports every half-hour because, in the Lima market, the term *drive time* often meant less than a thirty-minute commute and listeners were constantly recycling throughout the morning. When it became clear after a few years that a sports director's income in Lima would not be enough to support my family going forward, Tom was instrumental in helping me add advertising sales to my job description.

It was uncommon in that era for on-air talent to sell advertising, but Tom had challenged that norm by establishing good relationships with some key local advertisers to the benefit of both himself and the radio station. Advertisers bought the friendship and professionalism of Tom Francis as much as they bought WIMA radio, and Tom helped convince Les Rau that I could produce similar sales results.

Once I was given the chance to call on new advertising prospects, Tom's example of forming strong relationships with clients and making sure that their commercial copy was always correct and up-to-date was an excellent blueprint for me to follow. Using his example, I slowly built a steady account list and benefited from the fact that I rarely had to explain who I was or where I worked. Most business owners knew my voice and were familiar with my work on the air, so I rarely had to sell myself before selling the advantages of advertising on WIMA radio. While my sales success rate was far from one hundred percent, my growth in commission income over the years boosted my total annual earnings to a level that allowed me to live comfortably and spend my entire career in a sports market I truly loved.

One of my first clients was R.A. Flynn and Son Heating and Cooling in downtown Lima. Dick Flynn was the owner, and I convinced him to sponsor one of my morning sportscasts three days a week on a one-year trial basis. I told him I would write his commercials and read them live within each sportscast. I used a sports motif in his copy by identifying his business location as the "locker room;" calling his staff the "RHEEM team," in reference to the brand of products his company sold; and ending every commercial with an obvious but effective tag line, "And, you'll win with Flynn!" I began referring to Dick as "the coach" in these spots and within a few months, that's what half the people in town called him. This individual commercial attention helped produce solid business growth, and I was rewarded with a steady stream of annual advertising contracts.

After many years of hard work, Dick Flynn turned the company over to his son, Mike, and enjoyed several years in retirement before eventually passing away. To this day, R.A. Flynn and Son is a regular advertiser on WIMA. While Dick never

wanted to use his own voice on a commercial, I soon learned that
Mike was more outgoing and liked to poke fun at both himself
and me from time to time, so we switched to taping two-voice
commercials for the business and have used that format ever since
for all of his radio marketing.

While I owe Tom Francis much for my success in radio, the
WIMA audience remembers me most for broadcasts of high-school
football and basketball games, and the quality of that product
would not have been the same without the efforts of first, John
Barton, and, following his retirement, George Frazee, as my color
commentators.

John was the ideal radio analyst because he saw the games
through the eyes of a coach. While it was my job to tell listeners
what happened on the field or court, it was John's job to tell
listeners why and how it happened, and these are remarkably
different talents. On the handful of nights during our twenty-
five years together when laryngitis prevented me from doing the
play-by-play, John and I would switch roles. Suffice it to say that
I was as bad a color commentator as John was a play-by-play
broadcaster!

John Barton was born and raised in Lima, growing up on
the east side of town and eventually playing both basketball and
baseball at South High School. After graduating in 1954, John
enrolled at Ohio State University in Columbus and emerged in
1959 with a Bachelor's Degree in Education. His wife, Janet, was
also a Lima native, and they eventually became the proud parents
of three daughters, Cheryl, Shelley, and Sharon.

After college, John returned to Lima and spent his entire
career as an educator and, eventually, an administrator in the
Lima City School System. He was certified in health and physical
education and coached junior-high basketball for a number of
years. Playing golf and slow-pitch softball during the summer
were two of John's favorite hobbies, largely because drinking beer
was an integral part of both endeavors. He once told me that, in
hindsight, he was glad his early aspiration to become the varsity
boys' basketball coach at Lima Senior never worked out because

his intensity as a coach may well have led to a heart attack.

John and I immediately clicked as a broadcast pair, and he was so loyal to his part-time radio job that in twenty five years, except for health reasons during one season, I don't recall him missing more than five games. I never had to worry about John's calling at the last minute and telling me he couldn't make the game, and that was worth its weight in gold given everything else regarding broadcast preparation with which I occupied myself.

A few years after John and I started working together, George Frazee entered the picture. George was one of the most brilliant and diversely talented individuals I have ever met. He grew up in Pennsylvania but came to Ohio to attend and later graduate from Bluffton College, a school about twenty miles north of Lima now known as Bluffton University.

A brief glance at George's resume would reveal that he was a first-rate English teacher at Lima Senior, an amateur actor and director who spent several summers abroad with a troupe from Detroit performing classical plays in Greece, an insatiable high-school athletic official who worked varsity games in football, basketball, volleyball, baseball and softball, an adept golfer, and a voracious reader who could intelligently converse on virtually any topic.

George and John were friends through their city-school connection, and whenever George was not officiating a game on a night we were broadcasting, he'd volunteer to be our statistician. In the early years, those nights were rare, but as George's hereditary heart problems gradually took him away from the strenuous demands of officiating football and basketball, he became a more frequent member of our broadcast team.

In 1999, when John finally chose retirement winters in Florida over radio broadcasts in Lima, George Frazee took his place as my color announcer and filled that role eloquently until I retired. Whereas John had brought the vision of a coach to listeners, George brought the vision of a veteran official and was a handy sidekick to have when an unusual play or a rules interpretation needed further explanation.

While I have many fond memories of both men and the great times we had together during countless hours on the road, at ballgames and on the golf course, my most poignant recollection involves a September night in 1996. The venue was War Memorial Stadium in Ada, Ohio, and the event was a Saturday night local-college football broadcast of host Ohio Northern University and Bluffton College.

John and I were wedged into a small broadcast booth at one end of the press box, but George was absent because he had officiated a college volleyball tournament out of town that day. A steady rain was falling, and ONU was ahead by three touchdowns late in the second quarter.

When broadcast teams work together for many years, they develop a synergy where one person talks, then the other talks, and it happens effortlessly, without hesitation or eye contact. About two minutes before halftime, I described a play and instinctively paused for John to talk, but John didn't talk. I immediately sensed trouble, and when I glanced to my left, I saw John slumped face down on the counter in front of us.

I knew he needed help quickly, so I pretended there was timeout on the field and went to a commercial break. I immediately summoned assistance from ONU officials in the press box. John was conscious but could not communicate. Thankfully, football games have rescue squads standing by in case of serious injury, so the ONU officials summoned the paramedics, and they brought a stretcher to remove John from the press box.

In the meantime, I was back on the air describing the final two minutes of the first half. I didn't say a word about John because I had no idea about the extent of his medical problem. When the game reached halftime, I again went to a commercial break and told my board operator that John had become ill and was being taken to the hospital. I told him that I was going to abort the remainder of the broadcast and instructed him to return to network programming after the commercials and to say that we had technical difficulties if anyone called to ask what happened to the football game.

By the time I packed up my gear and was ready to leave the broadcast booth, I was a good fifteen to twenty minutes behind the ambulance which had taken John to Lima Memorial Hospital. I knew that John's wife, Janet, had gone with friends to the Lima Elks Club where John was expected to join her after the game, so before I left the press box, I called the Elks Club, explained the situation, and asked the manager to find Janet and tell her to get to Memorial Hospital as soon as possible.

When I finally arrived at the hospital emergency room, Janet was there, John was alert, and I learned that he had suffered a mild stroke. He was hospitalized for nearly two weeks and then needed the next two months to recover fully. Because George Frazee's officiating schedule precluded him from being a permanent fill-in on football Friday nights, I enlisted Bath High School's basketball coach, Mark Shine, to take John's place until his health returned. As the weeks progressed, Lima Senior's football team enjoyed its best season in school history and advanced all the way to the Division One state championship game at Paul Brown Stadium in Massillon, Ohio.

My happiest moment in broadcasting came on the last Saturday night of November, 1996, when John Barton was able to return to the microphone as my color commentator. Our brilliant station engineer, Mark Gierhart, designed a portable transmitting system that enabled George Frazee to become the first-ever sideline reporter on a WIMA game broadcast, and when the Lima Senior Spartans under Coach Leonard Rush won their first and only state title by defeating parochial-school juggernaut, Cleveland St. Ignatius, 38-30, it was made so much sweeter for me because John and I were back together again.

Unfortunately, all that remains today of these three special radio partners are my memories. John Barton lost a battle to lung cancer in February, 2002, at age 65. Although no male in George Frazee's genetic line had lived past fifty because of what he euphemistically called "bad plumbing," the miracles of modern medicine and two quintuple bypass operations enabled George to make it to age 60 before he passed in September, 2007. And

Tom Francis lived nearly eight decades before the advances of Alzheimer's disease took him at age 79 in March, 2014. Each of these special men touched me in a myriad of ways. They became more than just co-workers and men who enriched me professionally. They became true friends, the kind I think of so very often and miss so very much.

Life for each of us is a combination of ups and downs, of taking the good with the bad. While I had found the perfect job and was enjoying my place in a community that appreciated and supported high-school athletics, I was just five years into my radio career when I unexpectedly encountered the most difficult period of my life since the passing of my mother.

Life Happens

When Rosemary and I came to Lima in 1973, we were seven years into a marriage that had taken us all over the world and through experiences neither of us could have imagined back when we were two Catholic college students in the mid-60's contemplating the idea of sharing a life together. Additionally, I believe neither of us was initially aware of how significantly childhood circumstances influenced our attraction to each other.

Rosemary was the youngest of three girls each born five years apart and grew up in Zanesville, Ohio. Her father, Fred Bohn, as best I recall, showed little interest in raising daughters and spent much of his time away from home, either running his local plumbing business or traveling and rising through the ranks to become the Elks Club's national Grand Exalted Ruler. From my perspective, he was not the type of father a young girl would pick given the choice.

While I've already detailed the story of losing my mother at age fourteen, I really didn't realize the full impact of her death until years later. Marrying in one's early twenties was common in the 1960's, especially among Catholics raised with a strong prohibition against pre-marital sex. I didn't date much in college because I had little in the way of opportunities to meet girls. I was in an all-male classroom environment at Xavier and didn't even own a car until my senior year.

As I look back, when I did date, it was rarely about just having a fun evening at a movie or party. There always seemed to be a part of me wanting right from the outset to evaluate whether my date could someday be a marriage partner. As I discovered years later, not only was the main focus of my dating to find a wife, it was first and foremost centered on finding someone who would make a good mother for my children.

Reducing a complex issue to its core after many years of thought, counseling and observation, I've come to the conclusion that, in my opinion, Rosemary and I were both primarily looking for a good parent as a marriage partner and, in the rush that comes with the infatuation of young romance, we never gave much thought to our compatibility as adults. And the unusual circumstances we encountered during our first six years together in the military gave us little chance to develop that compatibility.

Between my time at Officer Candidate School and my deployment to Vietnam, we were separated for more than half of our first eighteen months as a couple. After nearly three years away from family and friends in Hawaii, there came the short stay in Washington, D.C. and the totally unpredictable outcome of my assignment to the Defense Intelligence School.

Most families with two young children spend Easter hunting eggs and eating Grandma's home-cooked ham. However, our first Easter after moving back to the mainland featured an 18-hour plane flight to an obscure country in Africa. And while our years in Ethiopia were both interesting and educational, they were hardly normal for two people from America's heartland.

If my hindsight view is correct and the quest to find a good mother for my children was at the top of my future-spouse priority list, I definitely achieved that goal. Rosemary's main focus was, is, and will always be her children, and she has always been a caring and devoted mother. In the years before we came to Lima, she shepherded Julie and Jeff through the challenges of a nomadic military life without complaint. And when I discovered the desire to make sports broadcasting my career, she fully supported the decision even though she had little personal interest in sports and had no way of foreseeing a work schedule that obligated me to a game broadcast every Friday night for seven months as well as most Tuesday and Saturday nights during basketball season.

Although we had decided that two natural children were all we wanted, we considered the idea of adoption but eventually learned that was not in God's plan for the Mullen family. About halfway through our time in Ethiopia, we came very close to adopting a young Ethiopian boy we met on a visit to a local orphanage. We had contacted the local authorities and filled out the required forms, but just when it looked as if the long bureaucratic paperwork process would produce a positive result, the child's extended family decided to raise the youngster and not put him up for adoption. The disappointment of that news coupled with the short time remaining on our tour in Ethiopia dampened our interest in pursuing another adoption.

After moving to Lima, Rosemary found an outlet for her nurturing, maternal nature by embarking on a career as a teacher whose main focus was helping students with special educational needs. Additionally, once we settled into our first home on West High Street, Rosemary and I volunteered to be foster parents, but after a year or so in the system and experiencing the challenges of blending other children into our family for short periods of time, we decided that type of work was not our calling.

As we grew into our careers, there seemed to be little time just for the two of us, partly due to my busy game broadcast schedule and partly because Rosemary didn't feel comfortable leaving the children overnight. And as fate would have it, when we finally attempted such an excursion, it ended abruptly on a bad note.

In the fall of 1977, I was able to get a pair of free tickets through the radio station to a Sunday afternoon Cincinnati Bengals game. After some initial hesitation, Rosemary agreed to leave late Saturday afternoon, stay overnight at a Dayton hotel with an on-site restaurant, go to the game and be home by early Sunday evening. A trusted neighborhood sitter said she would spend the weekend at our house with our then ten and eight year olds. The kids were looking forward to a movie video with popcorn that night, so we gave the sitter the trip details and hotel phone number and left on our weekend getaway.

After the short drive to Dayton, we checked into the hotel and were in the restaurant enjoying a nice meal when our waiter came to the table and said we had a phone call from Lima at the main desk in the lobby. We feared it was our sitter, and we were correct. She quickly assured us that Julie and Jeff were not in danger, but a house across the street was on fire and the children were frightened by the fire engines, the sirens, the visible flames and all the neighborhood commotion.

Needless to say, we abandoned our weekend plans, checked out of the hotel, and returned home as quickly as possible. As it turned out, smoke inhalation took the lives of the two small boys who lived in that house, and the trauma of the whole incident left a scar that greatly impacted any future thought of being away from the children overnight.

As the next couple of years unfolded, the strain on our marriage increased. There was a growing realization that we had few, if any, mutual interests outside of the children. We didn't socialize with other couples our age, and there seemed to be less interest in making time for each other. For a variety of reasons beginning with our adventure in Ethiopia, we had stopped attending church on a regular basis and our active participation in the normal weekly traditions of the Catholic faith was on the decline.

Sensing that our relationship was in trouble, we both agreed to attend group counseling, but after several sessions, Rosemary didn't feel comfortable in that setting and stopped going. I continued for nearly two years and learned a great deal about myself, especially how to better communicate my thoughts and feelings.

CHAPTER FOURTEEN

In 1978, we moved from West High Street to a home on
Wendell Avenue in Lima about ten blocks away but in the same
elementary-school district. It was a bigger house with more yard
space for the kids to play. While I was hopeful that the new home
would somehow help rejuvenate our relationship, by early 1980, it
seems we'd reached a breaking point.

During one discussion about our problems, Rosemary's
suggested solution was to stay married but live in separate
dwellings. In my mind, such an arrangement did not equate to a
marriage, so after months of inner turmoil, confusion, and some
latent religious hesitation, I returned home from Columbus in late
March from covering the 1980 boys' state high-school basketball
tournament and made the choice to move out of the house and seek
a divorce.

The next few weeks were the darkest in my life. I rented a
room at the locally owned Colonial Motel on Elida Road because
the discounted weekly rate was all I could afford. After leaving
work and returning to my motel room each evening, I would walk
about 500 yards to a restaurant and bar called the Buckingham Inn.
I walked there purposely so that I didn't have to operate a vehicle
after a few hours of drinking enough beer to dull my pain and help
me fall asleep but just short of enough to impair my ability to go to
work at 5 AM the next morning.

I was alone, hurt, scared and not at all sure what had
happened to my fourteen-year marriage. The enigmatic nature of
the breakup had many elements. Rosemary and I didn't fight. There
was no third party on either side trying to drive a wedge between
us. We were good parents with two healthy kids. However, we
just didn't seem to have much in common. I guess I couldn't deny
my feeling that her life revolved more around her natural children
and the school children she was teaching, and there wasn't much
interest in anything else.

There's an adage that things happen for a reason, and about
three weeks after checking into the Colonial Motel, a friend at
work, Kathy Stewart, who knew my personal situation well,
asked me if I would like to meet a good friend of hers just for a

drink. Kathy thought this friend and I would have a good deal
in common, and she suggested the meeting as a way to give me
something to do on a Friday evening other than drown my sorrows
at the Buckingham Inn.

I was reluctant to agree to such an idea so soon after my
breakup, but Kathy said she'd be there. Her point was, what harm
would it do to go out for an hour and have a drink? So, I finally
said yes, and after work on that Friday in mid-April, I drove to the
lounge at the former Ramada Inn location at Findlay Road and I-75
in Lima, where I met Kathy and she introduced me to Amy Freel.

During the next hour, I learned that Amy was a Lima
native with one son, Troy, who had just turned eleven. She was a
graduate of Bath High School and had been divorced for about a
year from David Freel, a Lima C.P.A. She had a good job, having
been selected as part of the start-up team by the plant manager at
Continental Plastics Corporation to hire shift workers for the newly
created production lines that would manufacture molded plastic
containers for Procter and Gamble's liquid detergent plant in Lima.

After about an hour of general conversation, Kathy said she
had to leave. I wasn't sure what to do because, while I found Amy
to be both attractive and interesting, all she was expecting was to
meet a guy her friend Kathy worked with for a drink. On sheer
impulse, as our gathering at the Ramada was about to break up, I
asked Amy if she'd like to have dinner together that night.

She said she would but doubted if she could get a sitter for
Troy. As we left the Ramada, the agreement was that she would go
home to check on a sitter, and I would go back to my room at the
motel and call her to see if dinner plans would work out.

About an hour later, I called Amy and, as expected, she had
no luck finding a sitter, and she couldn't take Troy to her parents'
house because they had gone out of town for the weekend. Since
going out for dinner wouldn't work, I asked if she'd be interested
in my picking up some carry-out food and having dinner at her
house. She said yes, so after getting directions to her place and
agreeing that Chinese sounded good, I picked up dinner and some
wine and headed for 145 Seriff Drive, a small ranch house located

behind the Westside Swim and Racquet Club off of Eastown Road here in Lima.

Kathy Stewart's hunch that Amy and I would have quite a bit in common was right on the money. On that Friday evening in April, 1980, we talked until four in the morning, and when I left to get a few hours of sleep before a remote radio broadcast I was committed to six hours later, I sensed strongly that a major change was about to unfold in my life.

Amy and I married almost one year to the day after we met and now, after well over three decades together, we thank the Lord each day for our many blessings, not the least of which was Kathy Stewart's intuition.

While I could spend many more chapters detailing the wonderful years that Amy and I have shared together and will revisit a bit more about our life together later, suffice it to say for now that with my personal life back on an even keel, I stopped those Buckingham Inn self-medicating sessions and reenergized my broadcasting career.

And, my, what an enriching next career chapter it became, one filled with some very memorable games as well as personal encounters with legendary coaches and an impressive list of high school stars destined to become great professional athletes.

Special Games

I n a career that spanned about three thousand broadcasts of
high-school and college athletic contests, there have been
many that are memorable for a variety of reasons. And, while I've
already detailed some games that stood out because of unusual
circumstances or because they were personal radio firsts, others
are unforgettable because they involved hallmark achievements
for local and area teams and coaches. But before reliving some
of those special moments, I vividly remember one broadcast that
could have ended my career in its infancy.

I go back to the night before the 1975 phone-line fiasco at
St. John Arena in Columbus and the eventual Saturday morning
Class A (small school) state championship broadcast I did with
Mick Acheson of WKTN in Kenton. At that time, the Class
AAA (big school) state semifinals were played on the Friday
night of tournament weekend, and the second game of the AAA
doubleheader that year featured two perennial powerhouses from
Northeast Ohio.

Cleveland Heights under coach Jim Cappelletti and Canton
McKinley under Spencerville native Bob Rupert were both 22

and 1. The trip to Columbus marked the thirteenth time Canton McKinley had made it to the state semifinals, but the Bulldogs had never taken home the ultimate prize, a championship trophy. This was the same McKinley team, led by senior Phil Hubbard, that had appeared in Lima two months earlier to take on John McCullough and the rest of the Spartans, and they were the statewide favorites to finally win it all in the big-school division.

The broadcast went smoothly and Canton McKinley led by eleven at halftime, but the Bulldogs managed to squander that lead over the last two quarters and ended up losing in overtime, 55-53. As the curtain came down on Phil Hubbard's high-school career and thousands of McKinley fans saw their title hopes evaporate yet again, the most unruly scene I have ever witnessed in thirty-one years of state tournament broadcasts suddenly erupted.

Those familiar with St. John Arena in the mid-70's remember that the players sat on gray sideline benches rather than on individual chairs that are used in today's college basketball venues. Moments after the game ended, a group of angry McKinley fans charged onto the floor from the courtside bleachers, grabbed one of the gray player benches, smashed it on the court and broke it into several pieces in frustration at now being an ignominiously perfect zip for a baker's dozen in their quest for a state basketball championship.

Several other McKinley fans charged after their head coach, prompting arena officials quickly to escort Bob Rupert back to the locker room for his own safety. John Barton and I were sitting shoulder-to-shoulder at courtside just back on the air from a commercial break and heading into our post-game show. We were doing our best to describe both the bizarre scene and security police's efforts to control the crowd when one irate McKinley fan came up from behind without our knowledge, leaned in between us and yelled at the top of his lungs, "Every f...ing year!" The remark was broadcast all over Northwest Ohio in a split second without any way to clip it or take it back.

Keep in mind that in 1975, FCC rules strictly prohibited the use of off-color language and a station could lose its license if it deliberately violated this sanction. No radio personality dared say so much as "hell" on the air, let alone use one of the world's most infamous four-letter words. Even though John and I had done nothing wrong and our station was merely a random outlet for one fan's foul-mouthed frustration, I envisioned complaints being registered with my boss the following Monday morning, a likely FCC investigation, and me possibly losing my job because of what had just happened.

Following the outburst, we quickly ended the broadcast, and John and I assessed the situation. We figured that by the time the "f-bomb" exploded, our audience was very small because, first, the game didn't involve teams from the Lima area and, second, because the incident took place several minutes after the final buzzer at nearly 11 PM on a Friday night. John and I were of the same mind, that our WIMA listeners who may have tuned in because of general interest, or the Phil Hubbard - Bob Rupert connection, had likely turned off their radios once the outcome was decided.

We resolved not to mention the scenario to anyone once we got back to Lima and hoped for the best. To my great relief, I never heard a word about it either from my boss, Les Rau, or from any listener, so both the station's license and my job were secure. In a noteworthy postscript, for the following year's state basketball tournament, the Ohio High School Athletic Association (OHSAA) changed its seating plan for fans from participating schools. Instead of selling them tickets for the bleachers and seats along the sides of the court, fans of the schools in the tournament were moved to the ends of the arena behind each basket. That policy exists to this day and makes it much easier for crowd control and much harder for a random expletive to find its way to an open radio microphone.

Before proceeding any further, an explanation of terminology is in order for reasons that will manifest themselves a bit later. When the state of Ohio held its first high school state basketball tournament in 1923, there were two classes of schools, A (larger schools) and B (smaller schools). That formula remained in place

until the 1956-57 school year, after which the OHSAA infused
a bit of political correctness and changed the classes to AA and
A following complaints by some small schools that, because
they were designated Class B, there was an unintended stigma
suggesting they were inferior rather than just smaller.

By 1971, the number of Ohio high schools participating in
athletics grew to the point where three classes were warranted,
so the big schools were renamed AAA, mid-size schools became
AA, and the small schools remained Class A. The change from
"Classes" to "Divisions" was made in the 1987-88 school year
when the OHSAA expanded its tournament format from three to
four separate groups of schools and dropped the letter designation
in favor of Roman numerals. The number of Ohio schools was
now divided by four according to enrollment size and schools were
placed, largest to smallest, in Divisions I, II, III and IV for most
sports. A few sports with less statewide participation still have only
three divisions while, at the other end of the spectrum, football has
expanded all the way to seven divisions.

Because spring sports are played during radio's revenue-
producing afternoon drive time and are subject to last-minute
postponement because of bad weather, I only scheduled high-
school baseball or softball broadcasts when a local team made it
to a regional final or to the state tournament. Although the number
of spring sport broadcasts paled in comparison to those in football
and basketball over my career, the small sample size did produce
some great memories.

Laura Ford coached softball at Lima's Bath High School
for thirty years before retiring in 2013, and, as of this writing, has
more victories (630) than any other softball coach in Ohio high-
school history. Coach Ford took teams to the state tournament
in Ashland, Ohio, seven times between 1987 and 2004, and my
WIMA microphone was there for each one. The Wildkittens'
most impressive run was from 2000 to 2002. Anchored by future
Cleveland State University pitcher, sophomore Grace Luginbuhl,
Bath defeated Portsmouth West 3-2 in the 2000 Division II state
semifinals, but fell 3-1 to Conneaut in the championship game.

One year later, the Wildkittens returned to Brookside Park, beat Benjamin Logan 4-0 in the semifinals and captured their first and only title the next day with an eleven-inning, 1-0 heart stopper over Poland Seminary.

A major difference between high school baseball and softball is how frequently and for how many innings a pitcher can be used. Baseball's overhand delivery puts considerably more stress on a pitcher's arm than the underhand motion of a softball pitcher. So, while state high-school rules limit baseball pitchers to ten innings in a seventy-two hour period, softball pitchers have no limits regarding innings or when they pitch.

While it may seem like a lot of work for one player, Grace Luginbuhl was now a well-seasoned junior and pitched both games of the 2001 state tournament. She gave up just one hit and struck out fourteen in the semifinal, and went all eleven innings scattering ten hits and striking out ten in the finals. That's eighteen scoreless innings and twenty-four strikeouts in two days for unquestionably the best pitcher ever of a storied softball program under Laura Ford, a consummate motivator and teacher who often isn't given nearly enough thought when it comes to Limaland's greatest high-school coaches.

In 2002, Bath was 28-0 going into the state semifinal round, but the Wildkittens' dream of back-to-back titles ended with a 1-0 loss to Cuyahoga Falls Walsh Jesuit. Grace Luginbuhl was such a dominant pitcher that, from the mid point of her junior year through her senior season, she won 46 straight before falling to Walsh Jesuit in her final high-school game. She also owns an OHSAA record that may never be eclipsed. Her career earned run average (ERA) is a miniscule 0.03, by far the lowest in history of any Ohio high-school softball pitcher with more than twenty career starts.

My top baseball broadcast memory dates back to June of 1976. The scene was the state high-school tournament in Columbus. Elida High School had earned a trip to state for the first time since 1958 by beating Hebron Lakewood 4-0 in the Class AA regional finals. Since the nine-game state tournament needed to be played in two days at Ohio State's baseball complex, half of the Friday semifinal games were played on the OSU practice diamond adjacent to the main facility, which was Trautman Field at that time.

That's where Elida's semifinal encounter with Pomeroy Meigs was assigned, but there was no press box at the practice diamond. I had to request a phone cable long enough to reach from the Trautman Field junction box to the practice diamond so that I could set up the card table and chairs I brought from home behind the backstop in order to call the game.

The extra effort was worth it because Coach Dick Prince and the Bulldogs beat Meigs 1-0 on a no-hitter by Rick Rumer. One walk was all that stood between Rumer and a perfect game. Meigs' pitcher, Jeff McKinney, was almost as impressive, limiting Elida to just one fifth-inning double by Jim Vandemark. However, the Bulldogs were able to get him over and get him in without benefit of another hit and advanced to the championship game against Orrville.

Although that contest was played the next day at Trautman Field, my broadcast vantage point wasn't much better. Since there wasn't enough room in the small press box for electronic media, I did the game from a top-row bleacher seat along the first base line. Craig Bowers started for Elida and pitched five hitless innings. The Bulldogs scored three times in their first at bat and enjoyed a 3-0 lead going to the top of the sixth. At that point, Coach Prince elected to bring back his ace, Rick Rumer, for the final two innings hoping to wrap up the title, but Orrville spoiled the strategy. The Red Riders got to Rumer for two runs in the sixth and another in the seventh, so the game was tied 3-3 as the Bulldogs came to bat for the final time.

Elida had the top of the order up to start the bottom of the seventh. Third-baseman Mike Sodders hit a ball in the air to right field that was misplayed for an error. The next batter, second-baseman Joe Scheele, attempted a sacrifice bunt but beat the throw to first for an infield single. Randy Prince, the Bulldogs' centerfielder and son of the head coach, also got the bunt sign, and

Orrville's defense was again unable to record an out, so the bases were loaded for catcher Roger Becker.

Since the small-ball approach had worked twice in a row against the Red Rider infield, Becker laid down a perfect squeeze bunt to score Sodders and ignite an immediate on-the-field celebration. Elida's 4-3 victory in the Class AA finals was not the first state baseball title in city history, but it marks the most recent one recorded by any of Lima's six high schools as of this writing.

While my top baseball and softball broadcast memories were easy to recall, it was a much more difficult task to cull through more than two thousand basketball broadcasts and somehow pare the list of great games and standout memories to a workable number. The process reminded me of a full-semester philosophy course I took at Xavier that was based on the single premise, "Choice is terrible because of what you have to leave out."

As might be expected, many of my best basketball memories stem from tournament broadcasts because of the caliber of play and the impact of those games on the schools and their communities. However, a couple of regular-season contests left lasting impressions.

Girls high-school basketball didn't become a fully recognized OHSAA sport until the 1975-76 school year, but the product quality and fan interest at most schools in the early years was limited. So, it took some time before the girls received any electronic media coverage in the Lima market. In the fall of 1982, I scheduled the first-ever regular-season broadcast on WIMA of a girls' varsity game because I knew the two teams involved would generate significant listener interest.

Gretchen Prichard was the original architect of the girls' basketball program at Bath High School and, by the early 1980's, she produced teams that could compete with anyone in her sport. Meanwhile, Fran Voll had built a similar program at Delphos St. Johns. In fact, his Blue Jay girls were so dominant that they made four consecutive state tournament appearances from 1977 to 1980 and won three titles.

The Wildkittens and Blue Jays played in different

conferences but met in a regular-season game in the fall of 1982. Bath was 7-1 and featured all-state senior, Lisa Bradley, who averaged nearly 27 points per game, plus two other seniors who scored in double figures. St. Johns was 7-0 and had four starters who averaged between 10 and 17 points per game. The game was played in Delphos and was billed as a big showdown between two local powerhouses, but the Blue Jays continually thwarted Bath's attempts to run their trademark fast-break offense, created nearly thirty turnovers, and, despite 35 points from Bradley, won going away 77-50.

Coach Voll took the Blue Jays to state tournaments in that season and the next before going on to become the head women's basketball coach at Bowling Green State University.

Coach "P," as her players lovingly called Prichard, won 485 games at Bath, including the school's only state championship in 1987. She coached nine eventual Division I players, including her daughter Amy, who went on to an outstanding career at Northwestern before embarking on her own coaching career at Ohio University, and was elected to the Ohio High School Basketball Coaches Association (OHSBCA) Hall of Fame in 2000. The Bath program didn't skip a beat when Greg Mauk took over as head coach following Gretchen Prichard's retirement, and Bath continues to rank number one in Ohio in total basketball victories in girls basketball.

As for the boys, when the head football coach at Ohio State University shows up in Lima for a regular-season high-school basketball game, there must be a special reason. That was the case in February of 1984, when Earl Bruce was spotted at the scorer's table in the Lima Senior Gymnasium watching two of his prize gridiron recruits play basketball.

William White and the Lima Senior Spartans were going against Cris Carter and the Middletown Middies in a Greater Miami Conference showdown in Lima. The Spartans were 15-1 with their only loss of the season having come earlier at Middletown 88-77 while the Middies were 14-2 but unbeaten in the GMC, so the game was a battle for first place.

The gymnasium was packed to the rafters, and the game more than lived up to its billing. Lee Stewart (21 points) and Melvin Walker (18 points) picked up the scoring slack for Lima Senior's best player, Anthony Thompson, who had scored 32 points at Middletown but was sidelined with an injury, and William White played lights-out defense all night. Cris Carter did score 24 points for Middletown, but in a game in which neither team led by more than four, junior guard Andre Reed (18 points) hit a jump shot at the buzzer to give Lima Senior the 70-68 win and a share of the GMC title.

Earl Bruce left the gym that night with a big smile on his face, knowing how athletic his two future Buckeyes were. Both became standout Ohio State football players, had lengthy NFL careers, and, in Carter's case, was elected to the NFL Hall of Fame.

I had the privilege of broadcasting thirty-one consecutive boys state high-school basketball tournaments between the years 1975 and 2005. All but two of them originated from the home court of the Ohio State Buckeyes. Twenty-two of those tournaments were played at St. John Arena with the last seven at Value City Arena. The lone exceptions were the 1986 and 1987 tournaments, which were held at the University of Dayton Arena because the city of Dayton outbid Columbus for the right to host the games during that two-year period. The venue change was not very well received, so the boys state tournament returned to Columbus in 1988 and has been there ever since.

Three of Lima's six high schools made it to state in boys basketball during my career, but none could bring home a title. Lima Central Catholic had the most opportunities, advancing to Columbus five times under OHSBCA Hall of Fame coach Bob Seggerson, but each of those appearances ended in heartbreak. Finally, five years after I had stepped away from the WIMA microphone, in his last year of a truly remarkable career, Coach Seggerson broke through in 2010 when he copped the long-awaited prize, this one in Division III, with a 60-57 finals victory over Orrville.

When I was behind the mic, twice the Thunderbirds advanced

to the championship game but lost by two points each time to
another parochial school. In 1989, it was Columbus Bishop Wherle
that edged LCC, 83-81, and in 1994, it was Youngstown Ursuline
that cut the nets after a 55-53 victory. On their three other trips to
state during my career, LCC lost in the semifinal round.

The most dramatic of those semifinal defeats came in 1992
when Berlin Hiland overcame a seven-point deficit in the final
thirty-five seconds and won 64-62. In that era, following each
semifinal game, fans of the winning school had to exit St. John
Arena and take their semifinal-game ticket stub next door to French
Fieldhouse to be able to purchase a ticket for the championship
game, and the first in line got the best seats.

After LCC scored with thirty-five seconds remaining to go
up by seven over Hiland, Coach Seggerson called a timeout just
to remind his team to forget about their comfortable lead and
play hard until the final buzzer. The timeout prompted hundreds
of LCC fans to scurry out of St. John Arena to get a place in the
championship-game ticket line at French Fieldhouse, figuring there
was no way the Thunderbirds could lose. Seggerson later told me
he never should have taken that timeout, because it totally changed
the momentum of the game.

Berlin Hiland's 1992 basketball story resembled an Ohio
version of *Hoosiers*. Here was a team of average-sized Amish boys
from a public school in 99.9 percent-white Holmes County led by
their universally loved and respected coach named Perry Reese,
who, almost unbelievably, was both black and Catholic. They had
lost only twice in the regular season and now, thanks largely to an
all-state senior, officially listed in the program as Jr. Raber, they
were in the Division IV state semifinals. Junior, as he was called,
and his friends were not about to give up, even though they were
down seven with less than a minute to play.

Thanks to a couple of quick three-point goals and some
critical misses by LCC at the foul line, Raber's Hawks found
themselves trailing by just one point on their final possession. The
Hawks got the ball into Raber's hands and, just as he dribbled
across the mid-court line, he launched a desperation shot with

one second left. The shot missed, and LCC thought they had won, but one official called what to this day in Lima is referred to as "the phantom foul" on LCC sophomore Salento Boddie, who had mildly challenged Raber's shot attempt by standing still with his arms raised straight up.

Raber, who finished with 31 points, calmly went to the line, made all three free throws, and Hiland escaped with a 64-62 win. The LCC coaches and players were devastated. The Thunderbird fans still in St. John Arena were stunned. Those already standing in French Fieldhouse were in total disbelief when Hiland fans started streaming through the door with news of the Hawks' miracle win and replacing them in the championship-game ticket line. Hiland's 1992 *Hoosiers*-esque story had a fitting ending the next day when the Hawks won their first state title 74-71 over Gates Mills Gilmour Academy.

The other two LCC state semifinal losses during my broadcast days were equally painful, but not nearly as dramatic. In 1993, the Thunderbirds fell to Fort Loramie 43-42, and in 2000, it was Jamestown Greenview that spoiled the day 51-50. Doing the math, LCC's five state tournament losses over that period were by a total of just eight points.

Lima Senior's boys basketball teams went to Columbus twice during my tenure. The first time was in 1982, guided by Spartan coach, Ron Niekamp. Losses at this level are always bitter, and this one was even more so when the Spartans fell 49-47 in the Class AAA semifinals to Cincinnati Roger Bacon on a widely disputed tip-in that many in the arena thought came after the buzzer but was signaled good by the officiating crew.

Lima Senior's second chance came in 1992 when Paul Whitney took his team to Columbus, and their semifinal opponent was, of all schools, Canton McKinley. In probably the most exciting basketball game I've ever broadcast, Lima Senior beat the Bulldogs 91-88 in double overtime, thanks in large part to senior Greg Simpson, who entered the tournament averaging more than 35 points per game and had just been selected as Ohio's Mr. Basketball and as a McDonald's High School All-American.

The Spartans trailed by eleven points after three quarters that Friday afternoon, but outscored the Bulldogs 28-17 in the final period to send the game to overtime tied at 78. The situation appeared hopeless near the end of overtime, with Lima Senior down by three and less than four seconds to play, when Simpson (34 points) made a desperation three-point shot from just two steps inside the half-court line as time ran out to force another four-minute session. The Spartans didn't score a field goal in the second overtime but made eight of ten free throws to win by three and advance to the finals against West Chester Lakota, a team from their own Greater Miami Conference.

The championship matchup marked the first time in history that two teams from the same conference met for the Division I title. Greg Simpson had a respectable 23-point championship game, but it was another Lima Senior guard, junior Demond Lyles, who scorched the nets for 43 points that day, including a still-standing Division I championship-game record nine three-point goals, but it wasn't enough. Lakota overcame a 12-point deficit after three quarters, forced overtime, and won 88-86. It was a loss that still rankles long-time Spartan fans to this very day.

The only other Lima boys team to reach the state tournament during my career was Shawnee High School. In 2000, Jeff Heistan's club had the misfortune to match up in game one against the eventual Division II state champions, Warrensville Heights, and fell in the semifinal round 81-70.

It's a bit ironic that, in a thirty-one year career, my only call of a state-basketball-championship victory for a local Lima team came in 1987, when the Bath girls won it all in Class AA. Coach Gretchen Prichard's club rode 21 points from Jackie Frye and 18 points from Kristin Holt to a 56-48 semifinal win over Tipp City Tippecanoe. In the title game, Bath (25-1) was matched against unbeaten Wellsville (27-0). Senior Kristin Holt's 29-point explosion provided half of her team's total, and Bath won the championship 58-55. Bath's girls have been to state five other times since 1987, but I was not a part of those broadcasts because, by the mid-'90s, we had a girls basketball broadcast crew at WIMA that did those games while I was occupied with boys regional contests.

The only other broadcast I did of a girls state tournament game was in 1989 when Lima Senior advanced to the Division I semifinals, but Cincinnati Mother of Mercy was too much for Ron Boedicker's Lady Spartans and ended their season 57-51.

While again not personally involved with the broadcasts, WIMA followed the Elida girls basketball team, coached by the late Vicki Mauk, three times to the state tournament in the 1990's. After losing in the Division II finals in 1990 to Garfield Heights Trinity, 70-60, and in 1995 to St. Bernard Roger Bacon, 64-48, in 1997, Coach Mauk and the Lady Dawgs finally brought home their first state championship trophy after crushing Vincent Warren 70-33.

In addition to all of the great memories involving Lima teams at the state basketball tournament, I was courtside to call the action for twelve state title victories involving boys teams from WIMA's immediate listening area. That list includes St. Henry (4), Marion Local (2), and Delphos St. Johns (2) as well as Kalida, Upper Scioto Valley, Lincolnview and Fort Jennings (1 each).

Three of those contests were particularly memorable because they marked the first titles for three exceptional OHSBCA Hall of Fame coaches. In 1979, Fran Guilbault of St. Henry won his first of three championships by beating Mansfield St. Peter's 64-57. Two years later, Dick Kortokrax of Kalida won his only title 58-44 over Gahanna Columbus Academy, and then in 1983, Bob Arnzen captured the prize he'd been seeking for thirty years at Delphos St. John's when the Blue Jays topped New Washington Buckeye Central 55-48.

Often, when the discussion comes around to which region of Ohio consistently produces the best basketball, Northwest Ohio receives its share of mentions. And, while, as has been said about all sports, it's all about the players, those who guide them are so vital to the game, and Limaland features three of the state's truly historically significant coaches.

Dick Kortokrax stands number one all time on the list of

career coaching victories in Ohio boys high school basketball with 850 and counting. Bob Arnzen ranks fourth on that list with 676 victories, and Fran Guilbault is ninth with 625. All three were consummate gentlemen to work with, brilliant coaches, and outstanding representatives of their communities.

While I enjoyed broadcasting basketball more than any other sport, and while basketball games made up the vast majority of my broadcasts, the circumstances leading up to one particular night, in another sport, at a venue clear across the state led to the most memorable game of my career.

The Most Special Game

" What was your most memorable broadcast?" Sports fans always seem to want an athlete, a coach, or, in my case, an announcer to boil down a lifetime of work into one shining moment. I've been asked that question hundreds of times and, perhaps surprisingly to those who feel shrinking such a decades-long anthology to four quarters of a single game's worth of action is an impossibility, I actually have an answer.

And, it's for that reason that I saved football for last in my compendium of broadcast memories. While basketball was my favorite play-by-play sport because of the challenge of describing the action and the constant ebb-and-flow of excitement, the one high-school broadcast that stands out above all others in my thirty-one year career is the 1996 Division I state championship football game.

Sure, the Lima Senior - Middletown gridiron showdowns in the early '80s with William White and Cris Carter were special. Sure, dozens of the annual Western Buckeye League pigskin battles involving local rivals Shawnee, Elida and Bath were first rate. Sure, three decades of LCC home games on Saturday nights showcased some terrific talent. Sure, hosting legendary football powerhouses like Cincinnati Moeller and Massillon at Lima Stadium were so very noteworthy. However, nothing was as exciting or memorable for so many different reasons as the night Lima Senior took on Cleveland St. Ignatius for the big-school football championship at Paul Brown Stadium in Massillon. But, of course, before there could be my quintessential broadcast night, there had to be a season.

Leonard Rush was entering his thirteenth year as head coach at Lima Senior in 1996. His 1995 team went 6-4 with a starting lineup of mostly underclassmen. The Spartans were projected to excel in '96, but how successful they would be was questionable because of their strength of schedule. In addition to seven tough games in the GMC, Lima Senior faced early non-conference road tests at Toledo St. Francis and Massillon plus a season-ending home game against Findlay.

Jimmy Morris was the talented senior quarterback. William "Red" Bratton ranked as one of the top running backs in the state. LCC transfer Nick Christoff led a versatile group of receivers. The Spartan offensive line averaged about 260 pounds and looked more like a group of small-college players than high-school kids. Linebacker Jim Barker, also an LCC transfer, anchored a stingy defense that gave up just 106 points in ten regular-season games. Barker was also an outstanding place-kicker with a field-goal range of up to fifty yards.

The 1996 season started on a promising note with a 21-0 win at St. Francis, but a road trip to Massillon the next week resulted in a 28-14 loss to the Tigers. At 1-1, the Spartans faced a critical home opener in week three against one of their most historically difficult opponents.

Cincinnati Princeton, which under legendary coach Pat Mancuso had sent its share of players on, not only to Division I schools but also to the NFL, had dominated Lima Senior on the gridiron from the day the Spartans joined the GMC in 1980. The Vikings won the first nine games, led the series 14-2, and had rolled over the Spartans 49-28 the year before in Cincinnati.

In one of the pivotal games of the 1996 season, Lima Senior beat Princeton 21-14 before a huge crowd at Lima Stadium and never looked back. After five more GMC victories - including road games at Sycamore, Hamilton and Lakota - the Spartans tuned up for the playoffs by crushing Middletown 63-14 and Findlay 57-6 in their final regular-season home games.

Unlike today's OHSAA format where eight teams in each computer region make the playoffs, only the top four teams in each region advanced to the 1996 postseason. Lima Senior was third in Division I, Region 2, behind Toledo St. John's and Troy and ahead of Springfield South. In most cases, regional semifinal matchups were seeded number 1 against number 4 and number 2 against number 3. However, because of geographic proximity and travel-cost savings, the OHSAA decided to pair Lima Senior against Toledo St. John's in the first round and have Troy play Springfield South.

The Spartans took on St. John's at Donnell Stadium in Findlay and won handily 24-7. On the same night, Troy scored all of its points in the first half and dispatched Springfield South 32-13. That set up a regional championship game the following weekend at the University of Dayton's Welcome Stadium. The game was a defensive struggle from start to finish. Lima Senior trailed 10-7 at halftime but rallied to beat Troy 13-10.

After the regional championship weekend, four teams remained in Division I – Lima Senior, Cincinnati Elder, Canton McKinley, and Cleveland St. Ignatius. Again, taking geography into consideration, the OHSAA paired Lima Senior and Elder in one state semifinal and McKinley and Ignatius in the other. The Spartans and Panthers had met on the gridiron nine times between 1980 and 1988 with Elder winning six of those games, but when the GMC expanded in the late '80s, Lima Senior had to drop a non-conference opponent, and the series against Elder came to an end.

The venue for the Spartans' state semifinal game was the same as the previous week, Welcome Stadium in Dayton. Game night turned out to be one of the coldest in my broadcast memory.

I was somewhat sheltered by an enclosed albeit unheated booth in the press box, but with temperatures below freezing and an even lower wind chill factor, the fans and players faced brutal game conditions. After a scoreless first period, Lima Senior recorded a safety, a 3-yard touchdown run by William Bratton, and a Jim Barker 39-yard field goal and took an 11-0 lead into the locker room at halftime.

The Panthers cut the deficit to three with a touchdown and two-point conversion in the third period, but Barker's leg came through again from 41 yards out, and Lima Senior led 14-8 going into the final twelve minutes. Early in the fourth quarter the Panthers tied the score on a 31-yard touchdown pass but failed on their two-point conversion attempt. With the season on the line, Spartan quarterback Jimmy Morris connected with Nick Christoff on a 72-yard touchdown bomb, and Jim Barker's extra point cemented a 21-14 Lima Senior victory.

In addition to making the state football finals for the first time in school history, Lima Senior's victory over Elder also put some pressure on longtime Cincinnati radio talk-show host, Bill Cunningham, to pay off a well-publicized promise. During the week prior to the state semifinal matchup, Cunningham boastfully told his 700-WLW audience that there was no way a team from Lima would beat the Elder Panthers. He was so sure that he promised to buy the most widely known product in Lima, Kewpee hamburgers, for the whole team if the Spartans won. The talk in town during the week after the win over Elder was as much about whether the often times bombastic and popular radio personality would honor his bet as it was about whether Lima Senior could win a state title.

Meanwhile, in the other Division I state semifinal game, Cleveland St. Ignatius, an all-male parochial school, beat Canton McKinley, 31-24, to earn its place in the title game. Ohio sports fans were not surprised to see Ignatius in that setting. During the previous eight seasons, from 1988 through 1995, the Wildcats' overall record was an incredible 104-4. They were Division I state champions in seven of those eight years. Their only stumble came in 1990, when they were number one in the computer rankings but were upset in the regional semifinals by Austintown Fitch.

Coach Chuck Kyle had built a program in Cleveland that resembled the one in Cincinnati from 1975 through 1980 when Gerry Faust and his Moeller Crusaders won five of six Division I state football titles. Now, five-time defending state champion Ignatius was pitted against the first-time state finalists from Lima Senior, and, predictably, very few pundits gave the Spartans a chance.

Having the opportunity to broadcast a state-championship game involving the primary public high school in the city that I called home was a great thrill, but two other game circumstances made the night even more special. First and foremost, both of my regular sidekicks were able to join me on the broadcast. John Barton had recovered sufficiently from the stroke he had suffered two months earlier and returned to the booth, and George Frazee traded his stat sheet for a microphone and debuted as a live sideline reporter, thanks to the ingenuity of our station engineer, Mark Gierhart, who made the use of a technique popularized on national broadcasts a reality for the championship game. Secondly, because the game was scheduled at Paul Brown Stadium in Massillon, Lima Senior had the extra motivation of returning to the site of their only regular-season loss, hopefully to expunge those bad memories.

And, so it was that David took on Goliath on a Saturday night, November 30, 1996. Mother Nature didn't help because a light mist fell for most of the evening, adding an element of dampness to the late-fall chill. The game started much like the pundits thought it would. Ignatius placekicker, Joe Zombek, who, I noted, in pre-game practice was kicking the ball out of the end zone from his own forty yard line, booted a 24-yard field goal to give the Wildcats a quick 3-0 lead. Ignatius got the ball back a couple of minutes later and struck from 44 yards away on a slashing run by their best back, Jon Blevins. All of a sudden it was 10-0 midway through the first quarter, and Spartan fans feared the worst.

Leonard Rush was not the type to panic, however, so he kept to his game plan of running William Bratton behind that big offensive line and mixing in an occasional pass. The Spartans drove into Wildcat territory and, just before the quarter ended, scored on a 27-yard field goal by Jim Barker.

As the second quarter started, Ignatius went back to work and methodically marched down the field. They got a 1-yard touchdown plunge from Paul Ardire, but the extra-point snap was mishandled, and the Wildcats failed to tack on the PAT. Perhaps that was an omen of things to come for the favorites from Cleveland. Although Ignatius had a 16-3 lead, Lima Senior's fortunes were about to turn dramatically.

On their next possession, the Spartans scored on a 53-yard pass from Jimmy Morris to Nick Christoff to pull the Spartans within six. The defense then forced an Ignatius punt, and Lima Senior proceeded to move the chains and advance the game clock very methodically. Just before halftime, Morris connected with his tight end, Domont Watkins, on a 14-yard touchdown pass, and Jim Barker's extra point sent the Spartans to the locker room ahead, 17-16.

As well as the Lima Senior offense had responded after trailing 16-3, Coach Rush knew the game's outcome would hinge on his team's defensive effort in the second half. The Spartans took the field in the third quarter with fresh inspiration and totally shut down the powerful Ignatius offense. The only score in that quarter came when Lima Senior's Jerian Butler recovered a blocked punt in the Ignatius end zone. Another Jim Barker PAT made the score 24-16 in favor of the Spartans.

The press-box scribes who had anointed Cleveland St. Ignatius as a prohibitive favorite really started scratching their heads when, early in the fourth quarter, Lima Senior scored again on a 21-yard run by William Bratton. Four straight Spartan touchdowns had turned a 16-3 deficit into a 31-16 lead, and the Wildcats were scrambling. But, in seven previous appearances in the state finals, the Clevelanders had never lost the championship game and weren't about to give up.

Ignatius served notice of that midway through the fourth quarter when Jon Blevins ran one in again from 28-yards out to cut Lima's lead to 31-23. Rather than sit on an eight-point lead and put the pressure on the defense, on the next Lima possession Coach Rush called a hitch-and-go pass play in a third-and-short situation, and the senior combination of Morris-to-Christoff hooked up again on a 48-yard scoring strike to put the game out of reach.

St. Ignatius scored once more, but when Lima Senior recovered the on-side kick, the Spartans ran out the clock, and the dream had come true. The Spartans had knocked off the five-time defending state champions from Cleveland St. Ignatius, 38-30, and brought back to Lima what, to this day, is the only state football championship among the six city high schools.

As I look back on that special night in Massillon, I'm proud to have been part of what I firmly believe is one of the best sports broadcasts in the history of WIMA radio. John Barton's insights on game strategy and his close association with many of the coaches on the Lima Senior staff added subtle details that listeners could find no where else. As for George Frazee, it was his sideline reporting that represented a technological breakthrough. With his background as an official, he was able immediately to explain any confusing game situations or penalties. Additionally, he was able to do live interviews from the field with Coach Rush and a couple of key players immediately after the victory, making our post-game celebration of a state championship extra special for the thousands of listeners back in Northwest Ohio.

The dethroning of the vaunted Catholic-school powerhouse from Cleveland was a huge story and, for weeks after the victory, Coach Rush received notes and calls of congratulations from other public-school football coaches throughout the state. It was as if the public-school David's slaying of the private-school Goliath had temporarily deflated the building tension between public and parochial schools over the subject of competitive balance in Ohio high-school athletics, which remains an issue on the front burner today.

I remember that game as if it had just concluded an hour

ago, as well as the beer-and-pizza celebration that ensued for several more hours at a small, locally owned motel in Massillon where a few Lima fans and the broadcast team had chosen to stay overnight.

A few years later, Amy and I were on a cruise in the Caribbean, and I wore my Lima Senior state championship tee shirt to the pool. A total stranger came up to me and said he was an alumnus of Cleveland St. Ignatius, and he told me the pain of losing to Lima Senior in the finals was still fresh in his mind. When I told him I had broadcast the game, he bought me a beer as a salute to Lima's success, which, perhaps, proves that, a win of that magnitude for those in Lima and a loss that big for those in Cleveland can echo for a long time.

Nearly twenty years after that victory, quarterback Jimmy Morris, now a middle-school assistant principal in the Shawnee school system, says the turning point in the 1996 championship season came in game six at Hamilton. "In the first part of the year," Morris said, "we pretty much followed Coach Rush's philosophy of running the football. But at Hamilton, he started to open up the offense and let us throw, and we won 31-3. After that game, we really took off and started to click." And click they did, scoring 193 points in their last four regular-season games.

Morris also credits the team's success to its unusual roster depth and experience. "We had twenty-two seniors on the team, very good skill players, a huge and deep offensive line, a nasty defense, and other than a couple of guys in limited circumstances, no one had to play both ways."

And, lest anyone is wondering whether Cincinnati's favorite radio loudmouth, Bill Cunningham, ever paid off his on-air wager, unlike some in the media who make such on-air wagers and then develop selective amnesia after they're proven wrong, according to Morris, he personally drove to Lima to attend the community celebration in the Lima Senior gymnasium following the state championship victory, spoke to the crowd for a couple of minutes, told them, "I'm a man of my word," and handed a check to Coach Rush to cover the cost of Kewpee hamburgers for the entire team.

There have been so many games, so many memories, all fueled by the inspiration and pride of a three-decade procession of student-athletes who, in all but a few cases, never played a team sport again following their high-school graduations.

However, in those few cases, there are certainly some notable exceptions, perhaps more than one would suspect for a play-by-play guy working in Lima, a town that, according to some, is an acronym for "lost in middle America."

Special Athletes

Let's be honest. My job was one that pretty much every sports fan would love to have. I got to pick the schedule of great high-school ballgames I was going to see each season for thirty-one years. When I arrived at the stadium or gym, I had a parking pass for a nearby space and a press pass to enter ahead of those waiting in line. While I never bought a ticket, I still sat in one of the best seats in the house. And, to top it all off, I got paid to be there.

If those weren't enough perks, I was privileged to call games involving a remarkable list of renowned athletes when they were just beginning to hone their skills as teenagers. Certainly many have asked me, "Who's the best player you've ever covered during your broadcasts?" But, to limit that answer to a single person or to one sport would be an injustice to so many other great athletes whose names and games I've called on WIMA radio.

In the process of covering the six local high schools and at least two dozen others in the listening area, there was a sizeable list of players each year who were good enough to continue competing at the college level, and these standouts contributed hundreds of memories to my mental highlight reel. The cream of the crop, however, was indeed a broadcaster's dream.

Since the majority of my play-by-play time involved basketball, most of the truly great athletes who intersected my career came from that sport. However, one of my earliest encounters with rare athletic talent after starting at WIMA involved a young man who, by the time he reached his senior year, found himself on the national stage in a sport that didn't draw nearly as much local attention at the high-school level as football and basketball.

Brad Komminsk was one of the best all-around athletes ever to come out of not only Shawnee High School but also the entire Lima area. He was an outstanding linebacker who many believe, including myself, could have played major college football. His size and quickness made him an efficient, blue-collar basketball player as well. In addition, I was told on more than one occasion that, had he chosen yet another sport, he may well have developed into an Olympic swimmer.

However, Brad's real passion and best sport was baseball. Jim Martz, Gomer native and longtime Major League Baseball scout, rated Komminsk so highly that the Atlanta Braves took him in the first round of the 1979 amateur draft with the number-four pick in the entire country behind Al Chambers (Mariners), Tim Leary (Mets) and Jay Schroeder (Blue Jays). Despite the lofty baseball draft pick, Schroeder opted for a career as a quarterback in the NFL, played 10 years for four different teams and threw for over 20,000 yards and over 100 touchdowns and actually was traded from the Redskins to the Raiders in exchange for St. Henry native and member of the vaunted Washington Redskins offensive line dubbed The Hogs, Jim Lachey. By coincidence, my own broadcast career intersected with Lachey, who, in the same way as Shawnee's Komminsk, was a rugged rebounder and solid starter on Fran Guilbault's undefeated state championship team in 1979.

I remember being in the newsroom at the Lima News along with Brad, his parents, and Jim Martz on the day the Associated Press teletype delivered the news of the Braves' first-round selection. Interviewing Brad that afternoon proved a bit challenging because media attention for high-school athletes in that era was uncommon, and I could tell he was uncomfortable trying to articulate his thoughts to a guy with a tape recorder who he knew only by his radio voice.

Brad Komminsk was blessed with the rare combination of speed, size and power. While I had seen him play many times on the gridiron and basketball court, his most impressive athletic performance came at a Lima American Legion state tournament baseball game at Ohio University. During that broadcast, Brad hit a home run that not only cleared the centerfield fence but hit on the rooftop of a two-story building that was located across the street that ran behind the fence. I'm not sure of the exact distance, but local observers who had watched baseball Hall of Famer Mike Schmidt's college career at Ohio University said they'd never seen Schmidt hit a ball that far, and here Komminsk had done it as a high-school player.

Brad decided to forego college, sign immediately with the Braves and start his journey through Atlanta's minor-league farm system. Just four years later, Brad had an outstanding 1983 AAA season at Richmond and was named International League Rookie of The Year. He made his Major League debut on August 14, 1983 and appeared in 19 games for the Braves.

The following spring, Brad had an excellent training camp and many thought he had earned a starting outfield spot with the Braves. But when the final roster cut came just before opening day, Atlanta manager Joe Torre elected to go with veteran outfielder Terry Harper and sent Komminsk back to begin the 1984 season at Richmond.

Although Brad did get called up and played in 90 games for Atlanta in 1984, he was never able to regenerate the momentum he had shown in the spring and hit just .203 in 301 plate appearances. He played in 106 more games with the Braves in 1985, but after hitting .227 and having a two-season strikeout total that averaged one every four times at bat, his days as a Brave were numbered.

After seeing almost no big-league action in 1985, Atlanta

traded Brad to Milwaukee, and over the next six years, he spent time with the Brewers, Indians, Giants, Orioles and Athletics. He was wearing an Oakland uniform during his final big-league game on October 5, 1991. After playing nine years at the highest level, Brad stayed in professional baseball for two more decades. He continued playing for several years in the minors before turning to coaching and then managing teams in both the Cleveland and Baltimore farm systems.

Following the 2012 season, after serving as the hitting coach for the Orioles' rookie-league team in Aberdeen, Maryland, Komminsk chose to retire from baseball to spend more time with his three teenage children in Columbus, Ohio, where he now buys and sells automobiles at the wholesale level for the Bobb Suzuki dealership.

While Brad Komminsk spent nine years in Major League Baseball and John McCullough remains the only player from Lima ever to see action in an NBA game, football is another matter. The city has produced a number of athletes who have earned a spot on a National Football League roster. The most famous of that group came before I arrived in Lima.

Joe Morrison played fourteen years with the New York Giants from 1959 through 1972. After starring in college at the University of Cincinnati, Morrison averaged 3.7 yards per carry as a professional running back but was more effective as a receiver where he totaled almost 5000 yards and 47 touchdowns and averaged 12.6 yards per catch. Perhaps as great a testimony as there can be for NFL players is their longevity. And, in a sport where the average length of a career is less than five years, Morrison's fourteen years is truly noteworthy.

While I never had the privilege of watching Joe Morrison in high school, I was able to catch a brief glimpse of his son, Rick, who was a multi-sport athlete at Bath High School from 1971 to 1975. Rick earned an athletic scholarship to Ball State University and played both football and baseball for Indiana's lone member of the Mid-American Conference (MAC). Under Coach Dave McClain, Morrison earned first-team all-MAC honors as a receiver in his sophomore and junior years.

In 1978, Dwight Wallace replaced McClain as head coach and revamped the Ball State offense. The Cardinals won MAC title that year, but Morrison's reception totals dropped significantly, and, as a result, he only made second-team all-conference as a senior. Rick also lettered all four years in baseball for the Cardinals and was elected to the Ball State athletic Hall of Fame in 1992 in both sports.

Morrison thought he'd have a chance to follow in his father's footsteps in professional football, but, despite pre-draft interest from several teams, his name was not called in the 1979 NFL draft. Rick ultimately signed a free-agent contract with the Chicago Bears but was released after playing in three pre-season games. Rick is now the Vice President of Enrollment Management at the University of Northwestern Ohio in Lima.

A third-generation Morrison is currently as of this writing showcasing his football talent at the University of Cincinnati. Rick's son, Max Morrison, had an outstanding career as a receiver in the high-octane passing offense at Kenton High School, located about thirty miles east of Lima, and currently stands fourth all-time in career receptions (293) in Ohio high-school football. Max was a starting wide receiver at the University of Cincinnati as a red-shirt sophomore in 2013 and will likely be moved to the slot-receiver position for his final two seasons as a Bearcat.

While I had little broadcast interaction with the Morrison clan, I was fortunate to have a 50-yard line seat in the press box during the early-'80s when four other future professional players were dominating the Lima Stadium gridiron. George McDuffie and Marcus Jackson were a pair of defensive linemen from Lima Senior who, after collegiate careers at Findlay and Purdue respectively, played briefly in the NFL. McDuffie saw action in three games with the Detroit Lions in 1987, and Jackson played in one game for the Indianapolis Colts in the same year.

Two other Lima Senior athletes fared better in the NFL. William Howard was a bruising fullback who played four years at Tennessee from 1984 through '87. In his junior year, Howard led the Volunteers in rushing with 787 yards. Following his time in Knoxville, Howard spent two years in the pros and made 21 starts for the Tampa Bay Buccaneers in 1988 and '89.

William White was a classmate of William Howard at Lima Senior. While he excelled as a combination running back/safety in high school, his college and professional career was spent entirely on defense. White started in the secondary at Ohio State as a true freshman, and after four seasons in Columbus played eleven years in the NFL. He was a fourth-round draft pick of the Detroit Lions but was immediately traded to Atlanta. After two seasons with the Falcons, White went to Kansas City for three years and then spent the final six seasons of his career back in Detroit with the Lions.

In addition to my many opportunities to broadcast these four Lima products, I also had the chance to call high-school games that featured several other future NFL players including Elida grad, Darren Reese, Cris Carter, Sonny Gordon, Keith Byars. Orlando Pace, Dan "Big Daddy" Wilkinson, Ben Roethlisberger, and the St. Henry High School trio of Bobby Hoying, Jeff Hartings and Jim Lachey.

Any broadcaster from a town the size of Lima would be blessed to have witnessed high-school performances of players like these, but in my case, about two thousand high-school basketball broadcasts over thirty-one years yielded an even larger and more accomplished group of prep phenoms.

The city of Lima alone produced not one but three players who earned the Associated Press's top award of Ohio's Mr. Basketball. Lima Senior's Greg Simpson was a two-time winner in 1991 and '92. Two years later the award went to Lima Central Catholic's Aaron Hutchins, and in 2004, to Shawnee's Jamar Butler.

While Simpson was a more dramatic player in many ways, Hutchins and Butler had better collegiate careers. "Hutch," as he was often called, was a prototypical point guard. He helped his LCC team advance to three straight state tournaments and then went on to an excellent Division I college career at Marquette University. The Golden Eagles' record book lists Aaron fourth all-time in assists (550), fourth in three-point goals (221) and ninth in steals (165).

Jamar Butler was another young man who raised coaches' eyebrows from the time he was in sixth grade. University of Cincinnati basketball coach Bob Huggins made frequent trips to Lima to see Butler play at Shawnee and recruited him hard, but when it came to a final college decision, Jamar signed with Thad Matta at Ohio State. Between 2004 and 2008, Butler scored 1,313 points for the Buckeyes, finished second all-time in career three-point goals (242), and second in career free-throw percentage (.868) with 231 makes in 266 attempts.

Since about two-thirds of my play-by-play work involved basketball games, it stands to reason that most of the names on my "memorable athlete" list come from that sport, and here's a stat that staggered me when I added up the figures. During my thirty-one years working in small-market radio in Northwest Ohio, I broadcast one or more games of at least twenty-four high-school players I can remember and identify who have totaled more than 186 years of playing time in the NBA and scored more than 125,000 points.

Those stat totals will continue to grow for several more years because topping that list of two dozen is Lebron James, regarded by some as the best all-around player in the history of professional basketball. I first saw Lebron play as a high-school freshman in the semifinals of the 2000 Ohio high-school state tournament. My first broadcast of Lebron came one game later in the state championship. He was 6'8" tall and weighed about 235 pounds, and it was clear from the moment I laid eyes on him that he was going straight to the NBA once his days at Akron St. Vincent-St. Mary were over.

James scored 25 points in the 2000 Division III championship game against Jamestown Greenview, the team that had edged LCC by one point in the semifinal round. Lebron's contribution, coupled with seven three-point field goals off the bench by another SVSM freshman, Dru Joyce, led the Irish to a 73-55 state title.

Akron SVSM advanced to the state finals all four years that

Lebron James played and won three championships. His only tournament loss in high school came in 2002 when, after two straight titles in Division III, the Irish moved up to Division II and fell in the finals to St. Bernard Roger Bacon 71-63. Lebron and company returned to state in 2003 in Division II and won his last high-school game 40-36 over Kettering Alter.

James, as of the 2013-14 season, has now played professional basketball for eleven years and has scored over 23,000 points. Barring injury and at his current scoring pace, in eight more seasons, Lebron will overtake Kareem Abdul-Jabbar (38,387) as the top scorer in league history. There were three other players I had the privilege to broadcast in high school who amassed five-digit NBA lifetime scoring totals.

Toledo Macomber product, Jim Jackson, played in Lima several times over four years against both Shawnee and Lima Senior. Jim later became an All-American at Ohio State and scored 12,690 points in a fourteen-year NBA career. Kettering Alter's Jim Paxson played in Lima against Lima Central Catholic and also led the Knights to the 1978 AAA state title 68-52 over Akron Central-Hower. After an outstanding collegiate career at the University of Dayton, Paxson played eleven years in the NBA and scored 11,199 points. The third five-digit NBA scorer who crossed my broadcasting path never played a high-school game in Ohio and did so only because he graduated from high school in the same year as Lima Senior's Greg Simpson. Before I get to that other player who has become a household name for NBA fans, a closer look at Simpson, arguably the most dynamic offensive player in Limaland basketball history, is in order.

The year was 1992, and Simpson had been named Ohio's Mr. Basketball for the second year in a row. The Spartans had lost a heart-breaker in overtime to West Chester Lakota in the Division I state finals, but Greg was one of twenty high-school stars throughout the country selected to participate in the McDonald's All-American game, which was held that year in Atlanta, Georgia.

Despite being just a bit over 6'1", Simpson was an explosive high-school player who could literally take over a game and carry his team to victory. How good was Greg Simpson? So talented that the Lima City Schools changed their athletic participation policy just so he could compete at the varsity level a year early.

In the 1988-89 school year, when Simpson was in ninth grade, Lima Senior was still a three-year high school. The city had three junior-high buildings that contained grades seven through nine, and the only way a ninth-grader could compete on a high-school varsity team was if that sport wasn't offered at the junior-high level. At the start of the '88-'89 season, it was clear Greg Simpson had the talent to play varsity basketball, but school policy did not allow it.

It wasn't long before pressure from several internal and external factions prompted the school board to reexamine that rule and, sure enough, shortly before Christmas, the board changed the athletic policy to allow ninth graders to participate on a varsity team if all pertinent parties concurred that it was in the best interest of the player and the school.

The change became known in Lima as the "Simpson Rule," and in January of 1989, Greg made his varsity debut against Middletown. Over the next three and a half years, he became the best and most exciting local basketball player I ever had the privilege to broadcast. Simpson still holds the city's single-game scoring record, a 57-point outburst against Toledo Start on February 1, 1992.

The opportunity to announce the 1992 McDonald's All-American game was one of my career highlights. It was the fifteenth anniversary of the event, and my wife Amy and I traveled with John Barton to Atlanta to cover the nationally televised Easter Sunday afternoon game. John Wooden, the UCLA basketball coaching legend, was the keynote speaker at the recognition dinner the night before the contest.

When John and I entered Alexander Coliseum on the campus of Georgia Tech University late Sunday morning to set up for our broadcast, we were ushered to our seats at a table just left of center court. The table to our right contained monitors and other electronic gear for a television broadcast. As I looked down press

row at courtside, it gradually dawned on me that, despite the fact
that twenty of the top high-school players in the country were
gathered for an all-star showdown, there were only two electronic
media crews doing live broadcasts that day.

One was the well-known team of James Brown and Billy
Packer of CBS television, and the other was the totally anonymous
duo of Mike Mullen and John Barton from WIMA radio in Lima,
Ohio. The CBS team was so impressed by the fact that one of
the players was being given hometown radio coverage that they
graciously acknowledged WIMA's presence during their telecast.

Greg Simpson, who had committed to play college basketball
at Ohio State, was assigned to the West team along with another
future Buckeye, 6'8" forward Charles Macon from Indiana.

The media spotlight on the West team, however, fell directly
on a 6'4" guard from Alameda, California named Jason Kidd, who
was considered by most recruiting services to be the best high-
school prospect in the country that year. And, given how history
would play out, the recruiting services knew what they were
talking about. All Jason did after a standout career at the University
of California was play seventeen years in the NBA, score 17,071
points, and then, in his first year after retiring as a player, in 2013,
assumed the position of head coach of the NBA's Brooklyn Nets.

Kidd was one of five West all-stars who scored in double
figures that afternoon. Greg Simpson added nine points, and the
West beat the East 100-85. Of the twenty players involved in the
1992 McDonald's All-American game, six eventually played in
the NBA. Tony Delk, Othella Harrington, Corliss Williamson,
Roderick Rhodes and John Wallace joined Jason Kidd in that elite
group.

Greg Simpson's first year under coach Randy Ayers in
Columbus went well, and he was named Big Ten Freshman of
the Year. However, personal problems eventually derailed his
college career, both at Ohio State and later at West Virginia, and
whatever chances he might have had to play in the NBA went by
the wayside.

The McDonald's All-American game is, as of 2014, now

thirty-seven years old, and there have been twenty-one Ohio players selected to participate. Sixteen were chosen during the span of my career, and I had the privilege to broadcast eleven of those sixteen in one or more regular-season or tournament games.

That list, in order of appearance in the McDonald's classic, includes Dwight Anderson (Dayton Roth, 1978), Clark Kellogg (Cleveland St. Joseph, 1979), John Paxson (Kettering Alter, 1979), Gary Grant (Canton McKinley, 1984), Jerome Lane (Akron St. Vincent-St. Mary, 1985), Treg Lee (Cleveland St. Joseph, 1987), Jim Jackson (Toledo Macomber, 1989), Greg Simpson (Lima Senior, 1992), Chris Kingsbury (Hamilton, 1993), Jason Collier (Springfield Catholic Central, 1996), and Lebron James (Akron St. Vincent-St. Mary, 2003).

Greg Simpson and Chris Kingsbury, once high-school foes in the Greater Miami Conference, were the only two on that list who never played in the NBA. Excluding games involving Simpson and Lebron James, my most vivid memory of the other nine players on that list goes back to the 1979 Class AAA state championship game. Clark Kellogg and his Cleveland St. Joseph teammates were matched against Granville Waiters and Columbus East. Both young men were headed to great careers at Ohio State and then to the NBA, but not before battling each other for a state title on their future college home court.

The East Tigers were loaded, with the seven-footer Waiters controlling the paint. The St. Joe's Vikings were pretty much a one-man gang led by Kellogg. East dominated the action from the start and led 54-26 at halftime. In the second half, Clark Kellogg literally tried to bring the Vikings back by himself and almost succeeded. Taking virtually every shot in the final two periods in an era before the three-point goal rule, Kellogg finished with 21 field goals and 9 free throws for a championship-game record 51 points. The rest of his teammates, however, made only 3 baskets and 8 foul shots in the entire game. Granville Waiters scored 15 points for East, but his supporting cast added another 59, and the Tigers held on to win 74-65. Although Jerry Lucas, while playing for Middletown in a state semifinal, once scored 53 in 1956, the most by any player in Ohio high school final-four history, Clark Kellogg's 51-point effort remains as of this writing the most points scored in any Ohio high-school championship game in any division, and I had one of the best seats in the house to see it.

Whether it was reliving the adrenalin rush of a single-game performance like Clark Kellogg in 1979 or just quietly musing over an obscure bit of trivia like being, to the best of my knowledge, the only radio play-by-play person on earth who has broadcast a high-school basketball game involving, albeit years apart, both Jason Kidd and Lebron James, I know that few in my position have been witness to the high-school exploits of such a varied and talented group of athletes.

As enjoyable as it was to watch so many gifted young men and women perform in their high-school sport of choice, it was for me equally fulfilling to watch the skilled coaching of such gifted athletes by some of the best high-school coaches in the state – coaches whose personalities and back stories were as interesting to me as the products they put on the field or court.

Special Coaches

Once upon a time, during my childhood years to be precise, sports were simply a collection of extra-curricular activities offered in high school. Athletic seasons were clearly defined and did not overlap, and students were able to participate in as many sports as time and their athletic prowess allowed. Adolescents' summers focused on part-time jobs and hanging out with friends rather than expensive travel leagues, open gyms and seemingly unending AAU tournaments. While winning was nice, losing was treated as an educational part of life rather than an unacceptable school-system condition in need of immediate repair.

Coaches and players put in untold hours and expended great effort for the love of the game and, for the players, the honor of wearing a varsity uniform. Coaches worked not necessarily for a better job at a bigger school, and players competed not just for an often-unrealistic chance at a college scholarship. There were no parent-run leagues in any sport for kids under twelve, and even when teenagers played high-school sports, parents were often too busy working and raising their families to attend all the games, much less openly stir the athletic pot with largely

uninformed opinions about a coach's philosophies or his overall
job performance.

And, for me, this type of sports landscape was still, for the
most part, the way it was when I began covering high-school sports
in Lima in the mid-1970's. However, significant changes were
looming and, over the next four decades, I saw the nature of youth
sports and the high-school coaching profession change profoundly.

From a student perspective, my children's generation saw an
increase in organized leagues at younger ages and a decrease in
multi-sport athletes because of growing pressure from high-school
coaches to choose one sport and play it on a year-round basis. At
the same time, parents became more involved, not only acting as a
daily taxi service for a growing list of practices and games but also
by becoming increasingly judgmental of those coaching their kids.

As we entered the twenty-first century, my athletic-minded
grandkids became part of organized teams from the time they
were in pre-school. One learned to skate before he was three, and
by the second grade was already on a travel hockey team. And a
steady increase of pressure to produce winning programs rendered
the varsity coach who starts and finishes a career at the same high
school a nearly extinct species.

While I have serious concerns about the direction and over-
saturation of youth sports and the associated effects that parental
and community pressure are having on high-school coaches, I'll
save that topic for another time and place. Instead, let me say that I
feel so very fortunate to have worked during an era and in an area
that produced so many excellent long-term coaches who were able
to ply their trade in relative peace and who were appreciated more
for their positive educational impact on student-athletes than for
their won-loss records. And, there are several so very memorable
to me whose domain was the crisp Friday and Saturday night air in
the fall.

One of the first coaches to appear on my radar screen after
arriving in Lima was Paul Greene. Paul was a four-sport athlete
at West Carrollton High School in the Dayton area and went on
to play college football at Otterbein. After twelve years of head-

coaching experience at both Huron and Dayton Oakwood high schools, he came to Lima in 1968 to teach mathematics and be the head football coach at Lima Central Catholic.

While the state high-school basketball tournament dates back to 1923, there was no state high-school football tournament in Ohio until nearly fifty years later. Beginning with the 1972 football season, the OHSAA debuted the Harbin Computer Rating System, which was designed to competitively rank every team in the state. The schools in each athletic division (AAA, AA, A) were divided into four regions, and the OHSAA plan called for each regional champion to advance to post-season play. That meant the ten-week football season was extended two weeks with six state-semifinal games scheduled in week eleven followed by three championship games in week twelve.

Paul Greene's LCC Thunderbirds were the first Lima team to qualify for post-season play in football. After just missing the playoffs by finishing second to Columbus Watterson in the 1972 Harbin rankings, LCC won Class AA, Region 6 in 1973 and played Cleveland Benedictine in the state semifinals at Massillon before a paid crowd listed at only 1,836 people. The Bengals kept LCC off the scoreboard in a 10-0 first half, and then returned two intercepted passes for touchdowns in the fourth quarter to complete their 23-0 victory. The Thunderbirds' only solace came the following week when Benedictine blasted Ironton 38-13 for the Class AA title. As most athletes will tell you, losses are perhaps a bit easier to take in post-season play when you lose to a team that wins it all. If you're going to lose, you want it to be to the best.

Paul Greene coached football at LCC for nineteen seasons and was inducted into the Ohio High School Football Coaches Association (OHSFCA) Hall of Fame in 2002. And, while there have been coaches on the high-school level who were more coach than teacher, Greene was certainly no one-trick pony. He was as talented a math teacher as he was a football coach. Additionally, unlike some of his coaching cohorts, he was media-friendly, which certainly made my job easier, since he always made himself available beforehand for an interview whenever LCC games were scheduled on WIMA.

    I clearly remember one such visit to his school office in the late 70's. LCC generally produced at least two or three players each year who were good enough to be recruited by college coaches. Coach Greene was always very realistic when discussing what the process of collegiate recruiting is all about and how high-school players should ultimately make their college choice. After one such conversation that he and I had on that subject, he opined that, "Kids should generally play one level lower than *they* think they can play, and two levels lower than *their parents* think they can play." It's a bit of timeless advice that, to this day, often goes unheeded.

    Jim Dally was another future Hall of Fame local football coach who was well established at Elida High School by the time I came to town. Unlike Paul Greene, who migrated to Lima as an adult, Dally was a Lima native blessed with generous athletic talent. In the mid-50's, Lima combined its two original high schools, South and Central, into one larger school, and Jim graduated in 1958 after playing football, basketball and baseball for three years at the new Lima Senior High School.

    Dally went to the University of Toledo on a football scholarship during a time when gifted athletes could still play two varsity sports at the college level. So, in addition to being a running back for the Rockets in the fall, Dally also played second base for UT in the spring. After earning a degree in education from Toledo, Dally became an assistant football coach at Columbus West for three years and then returned to Lima to be part of Russ Fravel's football staff at Bath High School.

    When Coach Fravel left Bath in 1967 to accept a head football job in Danvers, Massachusetts, Dally went with him. That arrangement lasted just one season, however, because Jim came back home in 1968 to accept the head football job at Elida, where he taught and coached for the next 25 years. A few years after retiring, Dally was inducted into the 2000 class of the OHSFCA Hall of Fame, making him the second Elida football coach to earn that honor. Jim's predecessor, Art Schreiber, was accorded similar

Hall of Fame accolades in 1997.

Working with Coach Dally as a sports reporter presented a bit of a challenge because Jim tended to respond to a microphone as if it were a rattlesnake about ready to strike. While normally very outgoing and a person who would gladly talk football for hours over a few beers, Jim was more than a little unsettled by the knowledge that his words were being taped for a radio audience. To Jim's credit, he never said no to an interview request, but I could always sense his relief when I finally hit the "off" button on the tape recorder. Years after he retired, Dally and I chuckled about those interview moments when, at times, it seemed as if a root canal might have been preferable. "The only person I wanted to talk to was you," he shared. "The rest of the people were covering rival teams, and I told them as little as possible."

Dally's football teams were noted for their tough, physical defense, and he was a high-school pioneer of the run-and-shoot offense, which is a freewheeling passing attack with an emphasis on receivers in motion and changing their routes based on what defense is employed. In 1982, Dally helped Elida achieve a banner year. A 6-6 tie at Van Wert was the only game that kept the Bulldogs from a perfect record, and they finished first in the Division II, Region 6 computer rankings. By this time, the OHSAA had expanded the football post-season to three weeks, allowing the top two teams in each computer region to play in a regional championship game prior to the state semifinals. In Elida's only playoff appearance under Coach Dally, they battled Toledo St. Francis at Lima Stadium but lost a 7-6 heartbreaker to the Knights.

Lima Senior had a number of head football coaches during my broadcast career, starting with Jerry Harris and Barry Blackstone in the late 70's and early 80's, but the Spartan coach I most remember is the man who led them to their only state championship in 1996.

Leonard Rush, a native of London, Kentucky, grew up in Hamilton, Ohio, and graduated from Garfield High School in 1965. He played college football at the University of Kentucky and lettered two years as an offensive lineman. Upon graduation,

Rush returned to Hamilton and was head football coach at Ross High School for six years and at Garfield for another three. Then, after a one-year stint at a school in Aurora, Indiana, and three years as defensive coordinator at Lakota High School just north of Cincinnati, Rush's longtime dream came true.

"I always wanted to be a head coach in the Greater Miami Conference," Rush told me, " because it was the best high-school conference in the state." Lima Senior had joined the GMC in 1980, and when the Spartans' head football job came open prior to the 1984 season, Leonard Rush was the first to apply. The search committee liked what they saw and heard during his interview and ultimately decided to hire him.

For the next seventeen years, Lima Senior football flourished under the no-nonsense leadership of Coach Rush. With only three losing seasons during his tenure, Rush's teams went 102-68 in regular-season games against some of the toughest competition in the state and were 7-3 in the post-season over the course of four years.

Of course, four of those seven playoff victories came during their 1996 state championship run. Prior to that, the Spartans made back-to-back playoff appearances in 1988 and '89 behind perhaps the most talented option quarterback in school history, Larmondo Watts. Lima Senior lost to Springfield North in the 1988 regional semifinals, but wins over Troy and Lancaster in 1989 set up a Division I state semifinal showdown with Cincinnati Moeller. The Crusaders' quarterback was future Pittsburgh Pirates outfielder Adam Hyzdu. After playing to a 14-14 tie in regulation, the game went three overtimes at Dayton's Welcome Stadium before the Crusaders prevailed 31-28.

Lima Senior's other football post-season appearance under Coach Rush came about under circumstances that were both bizarre and historic. In 1993, the Spartans opened the season 2-2 but won six in a row to finish 8-2. There was concern, however, about their initially announced fourth-place finish in the Division 1, Region 3 computer rankings. That finish, which made Lima Senior playoff-eligible, came about because the OHSAA issued a ruling in late October that another school in that computer region, Westerville North High School (WNHS) in suburban Columbus, had to forfeit two regular-season games because they had used an ineligible player.

The player in question was a sophomore whose parents lived in Kentucky but had sent him to WNHS because he had special-education needs. The problem arose upon the discovery that the student did not have an established legal guardian in Westerville and, therefore, was ineligible to compete in athletics according to OHSAA bylaws. When WNHS officials learned that the two forfeits had dropped them from second place to sixth in the final computer rankings, they hired an attorney to seek a court injunction to restore the two victories on the theory that OHSAA bylaws should not apply to students with special-education needs.

The WNHS attorney eventually persuaded a Common Pleas Court judge in Franklin County to reverse the OHSAA ruling and issue a Temporary Restraining Order (TRO) reinstating WNHS into the Division I, Region 3 playoffs. That ruling effectively bumped Lima Senior to fifth in the computer rankings and out of playoff contention.

When the initial playoff pairings were released by the OHSAA on the Sunday following the end of the 1993 regular season, the Spartans celebrated their opportunity to play for a state title. However, the news of the Columbus court decision arrived in Lima a day later, and the mood in the Lima Senior practice-field locker room turned from pure joy to abject devastation.

Coach Rush, who was also by then the Athletic Director at Lima Senior, was not about to accept this unusual turn of events without being heard. He and many others believed that a court should have no jurisdiction over a matter involving the bylaws of a private organization. So, with the backing of his school administration, including superintendent, Dr. Charles Buroker, Rush enlisted the help of Lima attorney, Matt Huffman. Mr. Huffman drafted a request for an injunction to stop the ruling by the judge in Columbus and filed it in Lima on Wednesday morning of that week.

Amidst significant debate in both communities over the dispute, and with the playoff game just three days away, Allen County Common Pleas Court Judge Richard Warren heard the matter immediately, and his decision a day later paved the way for history to be made in Ohio high-school football. In essence, Judge Warren ruled that, based on previous legal precedent, the court in Columbus should not have become involved in the matter because the OHSAA is a voluntary private organization with bylaws that all schools, as a basis of membership, agree to live by. He pointed out that establishing legal guardianship as a requirement for athletic eligibility was a valid OHSAA rule that had nothing to do with whether a student had special-educational needs. Judge Warren's order vacated the original TRO and put the matter back where it belonged, in the hands of the OHSAA.

With time running short and given the week-long saga and wanting to mend fences in both Westerville and Lima, the OHSAA, in Solomon-like manner, decided to have the two teams settle the matter on the field. This ruling meant that the eventual Division I state champion would be crowned one week later than champions in all the other divisions, but, for the only time in Ohio football playoff history, a Sunday afternoon play-in game was ordered between Lima Senior and Westerville North at Marion Harding High School.

WIMA normally carried Cincinnati Bengals broadcasts on fall Sunday afternoons, but this unique playoff game involving Lima Senior could not be ignored. I called the telephone company in Marion and, after explaining the unusual situation, they honored my after-order-deadline request to install a broadcast line in the Marion Harding press box.

John Barton and I made the drive to Marion that Sunday and, instead of hearing an NFL game, WIMA listeners heard the reenergized Spartans prove that they deserved their post-season berth by knocking off the Warriors 20-14. driving nearly sixty yards in the final three minutes in the rain for the winning touchdown. Meanwhile, Mt. Vernon High School, who had expected to play either Lima Senior or Westerville North in week one of the playoffs, had to wait an extra week before taking on the Spartans on Saturday, November 20, at Dublin Coffman Stadium. However, a missed extra point was the difference in that game and Lima Senior's season came to an end 21-20.

Leonard Rush retired as head football coach at Lima Senior after the 2000 season, and five years later, as a tribute to his long and successful career at three different Ohio high schools, he was inducted into the OHSFBC Hall of Fame.

Coach Rush was a quiet man away from football. He was not one to socialize much with other coaches, teachers, or radio broadcasters for that matter, but he was a fiercely dedicated individual. He viewed every young man who played for him as special. Whether you were the star quarterback or the number-five tackle on the defensive line, every Lima Senior football player knew that Coach Rush appreciated his contribution to the team and would help him in any way possible both on and off the field. Rush's dedication and loyalty to his players and assistant coaches earned their respect and loyalty a thousand times over. Leonard and his wife, Linda, are now enjoying their retirement years in Florida.

Paul Greene – Jim Dally – Leonard Rush – all three of these gentlemen were accomplished athletes in high school and college before embarking on successful careers as high-school coaches. However, there was another memorable football coach, the longtime leader of the Bath Wildcats, Gary DeLuca, who came to the profession from a slightly different direction.

Although Gary played football at Sandy Valley High School in Canton, Ohio, and continued his gridiron career at Wilmington College, he described himself to me as no more than "a member of the team" in his one year there. DeLuca also lettered in track at Wilmington and specialized in distance running. After transferring as a sophomore to Ohio University because it was a less expensive collegiate option, DeLuca gave up varsity athletics and competed in gymnastics as a club sport. Despite the cessation of his collegiate varsity athletic involvement, he never lost his love for the game of football or his desire to coach that sport.

After graduating from Ohio University in 1967 with a degree

in education, DeLuca spent time on four different high-school football staffs in northeast Ohio, including four years as head coach at Maple Heights, before accepting a position at Bath High School in Lima in 1980 as a health and physical education teacher and head football coach.

In addition to being an excellent teacher and motivator, DeLuca had an uncanny ability to accomplish something that is extremely difficult to do at the high-school level. He was, in my opinion, the best I ever saw at making half-time adjustments that significantly impacted the outcome of many of the Bath games I broadcast.

The best example of that came during the final regular season game of the 1985 season. The Wildcats stood 9-0 and needed a road victory at Van Wert to win the outright Western Buckeye League title. The Cougars were 8-1 and could share the WBL title by beating Bath. Because of the implications of the outcome, I canceled WIMA's original plan to broadcast the annual Shawnee-Elida gridiron showdown and scheduled Bath at Van Wert as our Friday night showcase game for week ten.

Van Wert played an almost perfect first half and looked virtually unstoppable as they took a 19-0 halftime lead into their home locker room. I don't know what Coach DeLuca did or said, but while the two school bands entertained the crowd for fifteen minutes, he made several offensive and defensive adjustments and got his players and staff to buy into the changes. The Wildcats were a totally different team in the second half and fought back to win 24-19. The victory secured an outright WBL championship, and the only perfect regular season in the DeLuca era.

In his thirteen seasons at Bath, his teams posted a record of 87-42-1 and made the playoffs in five of those thirteen years. The first trip to the post-season in Bath history came in 1984 following a 9-1 regular season. This was the last year before the next OHSAA football playoff expansion, so only two teams in each computer region advanced to the post-season. That meant a road trip for number-two seed Bath to Elyria's Ely Stadium to take on top-seeded Elyria Catholic in the Division III, Region 10 championship.

I'll never forget the night of that broadcast. A driving rain/ sleet mixture throughout the game turned the field into a quagmire. As the visiting team, Bath wore white jerseys with Columbia Blue numerals and lettering. So, by the middle of the first quarter, figuring out who had the football was nearly impossible because mud on the white jerseys and light blue numbers made them unreadable even with binoculars for either my broadcast partner John Barton or me. Elyria Catholic wore dark green jerseys with white numbers, but they too became illegible as the game continued.

In addition to the rain and the muddy field, the window in the visitor's radio booth at Ely Stadium was a solid piece of Plexiglas and, because of the temperature differential between the inside and outside, the Plexiglas fogged up continuously throughout the game. Someone provided me with an old bath towel, and after each play, I wiped off the Plexiglas as best I could in hopes of discerning which mud-covered players were involved in the action. When time finally expired after four quarters, Elyria Catholic slogged away with a 7-6 win and one of the most challenging nights of my broadcast career was over.

Coach Deluca's Bath teams also made the playoffs in 1985, '88, '89 and 1992, when they went all the way to the Division III state semifinals before losing to a Mentor Lake Catholic squad that featured two future stars who would also challenge for a spot on my lifetime "all-name" team.

In what turned out to be Gary DeLuca's last game as head coach at Bath, a talented running back named Carmen Ilaqua scored five straight touchdowns against the Wildcats, and Lake Catholic won easily 42-13. Ilaqua pursued an Ivy League education and became captain of the football team at Yale University.

Joe Jureviscius was a wide receiver for the Cougars and later played for Joe Paterno at Penn State University and was a second-round draft choice of the New York Giants in 1998. After eleven seasons in the NFL with the Giants, Tampa Bay, Seattle and the Cleveland Browns, his career ended because of a staph infection he developed following knee surgery in late 2008. After being released by the Browns before training camp in 2009, Jurevicious filed a lawsuit against the team for failure to properly sterilize its training facility in Berea, Ohio, and also against two doctors at the Cleveland Clinic for failure to take proper precautions against infection. Both the Browns and the Cleveland Clinic settled confidentially with Jurevicious in 2010.

Gary DeLuca decided not to coach anymore after the 1992 season and spent the rest of his career in education as an administrator in the Findlay, Shawnee, and Allen East school districts. The man who succeeded him as head coach at Bath turned out to be one of the most colorful and, at times, controversial coaches I ever had the privilege of covering.

Jerry Cooper was the youngest of ten children and excelled in three different sports at Mt. Gilead High School in Morrow County. He was recruited to play football at Otterbein College but suffered a knee injury in his freshman year. Although his playing days were curtailed, his passion for football led him to serve as a volunteer high-school coach while he completed his college education.

After graduation, he became a graduate assistant coach at Otterbein for two seasons, spent one year as head coach at Lucas High School, went back to college for the next three years as an assistant at Kenyon College, and then returned to the high-school ranks.

Cooper was head football coach at Waynesfield-Goshen High School in 1988 and '89 and at Hicksville from 1990 through '92. When Gary DeLuca stepped down at Bath after the '92 season, Jerry Cooper was brought in as his replacement, and he guided the Wildcat program for the next seven years.

For many years, WIMA's first high-school football broadcast of the season was Allen East against Bath. The series started in 1987 as a non-conference opener for each school, and it contained plenty of backyard-rivalry intensity, since the two school districts sit side-by-side and most of the players knew each other well. My first pre-game interview with Jerry Cooper came the day before

Bath's 1993 season opener against the Mustangs, and it's one I will never forget.

I had been in countless football coaches' offices by that time in my career and was used to varying degrees of clutter, equipment and old jerseys lying around. When I stepped into Jerry Cooper's office in the Bath Stadium locker room, I thought I was in the wrong place.

The room was ready for a military-type inspection. His desktop was immaculate with not even so much as a paper-clip out of place. On the wall was a large bulletin board with ten sheets of paper neatly stapled to the board in two rows of five. Each sheet contained the neatly lettered name of one of Bath's ten regular-season opponents along with a variety of statistical information about that team. The sheets were stapled in the order the games were to be played that fall.

Behind Cooper's desk was a metal-shelf unit that contained neatly labeled videotapes standing side-by-side in chronological order. There were tapes of every Bath game for the past three seasons. I worked with Jerry Cooper for the next thirteen years as he coached teams at Bath, Columbus Grove and LCC and can unequivocally say he was the most organized, detailed, and media-helpful coach I ever encountered.

In his seven years at Bath, Cooper's teams went 42-28 and made the playoffs three times in the always-competitive Western Buckeye League. In 2000, Cooper saw a golden opportunity both athletically and professionally and moved from Bath to the head football job at Columbus Grove, a smaller Putnam County school about fifteen miles north of Lima.

That job was open because Coach Mike Fell, who had built the Bulldogs into a perennial powerhouse in the Northwest Conference, had moved to a bigger school (Celina) in the Western Buckeye League. From 1997 through '99, Columbus Grove's regular-season football record was an outstanding 28-2.

Jerry Cooper picked up right where Mike Fell left off, and in the five seasons he coached at Columbus Grove, the Bulldogs won 45 of 50 regular season games, made the playoffs every year, and won the Division VI state championship in 2003 behind the relentless running of Blaine Maag, who later would go on to a very successful coaching career in track, first at Grand Valley State University and, as of this writing, at Michigan State.

I broadcast most of those playoff games, and when I drove to Columbus Grove a day or two ahead of each contest to do my pre-game tape with Coach Cooper, he'd welcome me with a fresh manila file folder filled with everything I could possibly need for the broadcast.

There were depth charts not only for his team but for their playoff opponent as well. There were rosters and stat sheets for both teams and a playoff history for each school. It was the detailed homework that Cooper had done for himself and his coaching staff, but he graciously passed copies along to me, and I always appreciated it.

Jerry Cooper was always a man in search of a new challenge so, in 2005, he left Columbus Grove for the head football job at Lima Central Catholic, stayed there through the 2013 campaign, won five Northwest Conference football championships, and took the Thunderbirds to the playoffs eight times in nine seasons.

The wanderlust and new-challenge bug cropped up again following the 2013 season, so after filing for his pension from the Ohio State Teachers Retirement System, Jerry and his family headed for Seymour, Tennessee, and another opportunity to coach high-school football.

While Cooper's extremely competitive personality grated at times on his coaching peers and, I'm sure, on more than one area football official, I have seen plenty of evidence that he worked tirelessly to mold his players into solid, upstanding young men and, when he becomes eligible, will, in my opinion, take his place in the OHSFCA Hall of Fame.

I was blessed to occasionally work with several other top-notch high school football coaches in the area during my career, including but certainly not limited to Mike Mauk at Kenton, Bill Goodwin at Allen East, Todd Schulte at Delphos St. Johns, Eugene "Skip" Baughman at St. Marys, Dennis Lee at Bluffton, and Mike

Fell at Columbus Grove, Celina, Ada and now Lima Senior.

However, much like the way that stadiums grow silent in late fall and gymnasiums come to life, it's time now to hit the football fade button and rekindle some memories of my favorite coaches from the world of basketball and other sports.

Hall of Famers

Just as I missed out on seeing great athletes like Joe Morrison, Joe Fisher, Jeff Miller and others who made their mark in local sports before I came to Lima, I also missed being here during the glory years of coaches like Seraph Pope, Jim Young and Don Penhorwood, who became household names in this community because of their dedication to enriching the lives of young people through athletics.

Another in that group was Joe Bowers, who spent his entire career teaching and coaching in the Lima City School system. Joe was a coaching jack-of-all-trades at many levels but is most remembered for his work as the head baseball coach at Lima Senior. During Bowers' long and illustrious career, his time at Lima Senior from 1960 through 1964 could be described as his coaching zenith. In that five-year period, the Spartans made five straight trips to the Class AA state tournament. After one semifinal loss and three runner-up trophies in the first four tries, Coach Bowers led Lima Senior to an undefeated season and the ultimate prize, the state baseball title, in 1964 with an 8-2 win over Lancaster in the semifinals and a nine-inning 7-6 triumph over Cleveland Benedictine in the finals. Long-time Spartan fans will, no doubt, remember Roger Doty's Baltimore chop and Davey Reynolds' mad dash for home with the run that made Lima Senior king of the diamond back in '64.

Bowers retired from coaching in 1975, just after I had started at WIMA. John Barton and others had regaled me with many Joe Bowers stories, and I looked forward to telephoning him from the newsroom to record an interview about his career and retirement plans. As I soon learned, however, talking to Joe Bowers resembled talking to a guy like Yogi Berra, who has always been known for his elocutionary meanderings, misspeaks and malapropisms.

Joe was such a stream-of-consciousness thinker and talker that I literally had trouble finding a fifteen-second audio clip to use out of a twenty-minute taped conversation because Joe's answers to my questions bounced back and forth from topic to topic like a silver sphere in an old-time pinball machine. Joe Bowers must have been a very special coach, however, because those who played for him loved him like a father and relished talking about the lessons they learned under his tutelage.

Just one example of that is a man named Jim Tobin. Jim was a Spartan baseball player in the 1960's who went on to become the CEO of Boston Scientific, a multi-billion dollar company in Massachusetts with more than 25,000 employees that makes artificial heart valves for the medical profession.

When the new Lima Senior complex was under construction in the early 2000's, he wanted to do something to make sure no one in Lima ever forgot his high school baseball coach. Mr. Tobin made only one stipulation when he promised to donate the more than $325,000 necessary to make sure the new baseball diamond on campus was state-of-the-art in every way. He insisted that the facility be named Joe Bowers Field. When it comes to the Lima sports scene, there are few who ever coached that cast a longer shadow than Coach Bowers.

Joe is one of three men from Lima who have been elected to the Ohio High School Baseball Coaches Association Hall of Fame. The other two are Dick Prince, who coached and directed

the athletic program at Elida for many years and led the Bulldogs
to the state title in 1976, and Phil Krouskop, whose teams amassed
more than 500 wins during his thirty-nine years as head baseball
coach at Perry High School in Lima.

The Ohio Softball Coaches Hall of Fame also includes three
local names. The most recent addition was Laura Ford, who, as of
this writing, has more victories (630) than any other coach in Ohio
softball history and whose accomplishments at Bath High School
I was privileged to follow. The other two women in this category
earned most of their stripes before my broadcasting career began.

Bernadine "Bernie" Rinehardt was the initial architect of
the girls' athletic program at Shawnee High School. A native of
Deshler, Ohio, and a graduate of Bowling Green State University,
Rinehardt taught health and physical education at Shawnee from
1953 to 1986. She was instrumental in starting both intramural and
varsity female athletic programs and, at various times, coached
volleyball, basketball and softball for the Indians. She was a
rated high school official in volleyball and softball, and today, the
school's outdoor athletic complex bears her name.

Dorothy Edwards graduated from Elida High School in 1952,
and after earning a degree in education from Findlay College,
came back to Elida and spent the next forty-seven years of her
life teaching and coaching. She was the first head coach in six
different girls' sports at Elida but spent most of her coaching time
in volleyball and softball. While I had little broadcast interaction
with Dorothy, I admired her tenacity and willingness to advance
the cause of girls' athletics in any manner possible. As a tribute to
her life-long contribution to the community, Elida school officials
renamed the softball field Dorothy Edwards Field.

Before recounting recollections of some of the great
basketball coaches with whom I had the privilege to work, I want
to acknowledge two other longtime local mentors in the sport in
which I lettered at Xavier. Ron Huber was an outstanding tennis
coach for many years at Shawnee High School. His teams won
numerous Western Buckeye League titles, and one of his protégés,
Justin O'Neal, was a three-time state singles champion in 1993,

'95 and '96. Ron also worked alongside me during the 1974 tennis
tournament that WLIO televised from the Westside Swim and
Racquet Club in Lima and has been a friend and, at times, neighbor
ever since.

Another longtime friend and local tennis coach, Denny
Schwinnen, recently retired after thirty-six years at Elida High
School. His Bulldogs also produced several WBL championships,
and two Elida doubles teams brought home state championship
trophies. Pierre Tanguay and Mike Fraley won the A-AA title
in 1979 and the tandem of Landon Neuman and Jayson Hilborn
captured the 2005 Division II state championship.

In August, 2013, Elida High School saluted Schwinnen's
coaching career by naming the school tennis courts in his honor.
Both Denny Schwinnen and Ron Huber were 2010 inductees into
the Ohio High School Tennis Coaches Association Hall of Fame.

I saved my basketball coaches' recollections for last because
their sheer numbers found me, once again, in my collegiately
inspired philosophical quandary of "choice is terrible because of
what you have to leave out." Since the majority of my basketball
broadcasts involved boys teams from Lima Senior, LCC, Elida,
Bath and Shawnee, most of my interaction was with that group
of coaches, but there were many others throughout the area who
contributed to my lifetime basketball mosaic.

When people today attend basketball games at Delphos St.
Johns High School, they purchase tickets for seats in the Robert
A. Arnzen Gymnasium, an aptly named facility that honors the
man who coached basketball for forty-three years at DSJ and
won seventy percent of his games (676-271). Coach Arnzen was
twenty-five years into his career and already a local legend when I
arrived in Lima.

For many years there were two special dates on my WIMA
basketball broadcast schedule. They were the Sunday afternoon
home-and-home showdowns between the county's two parochial
powerhouses, Delphos St. Johns and Lima Central Catholic. When
I talked with Coach Arnzen before those games, I soon learned that
he rarely, if ever, scouted an opponent.

He believed strongly in teaching and then practicing his formula for both offensive and defensive basketball. If his players executed his system, and were both fundamentally sound and in top physical condition, he believed they could compete with any team regardless of the opposition's size, talent level or experience. His record confirms the validity of his philosophy. In a time when so many of his peers sought every possible means to learn opponents' tendencies, how unique Coach Arnzen's approach was.

The Ohio High School Basketball Coaches Association (OHSBCA) started their Hall of Fame in 1987 and, appropriately because of the success and longevity of his career, Bob Arnzen was the first coach from this area to be inducted in 1995. Since that time, eight more coaches who crossed my broadcast path have earned the same honor. The OHSBCA class of 1996 included Ray Etzler, who spent his entire career at Crestview High School in the village of Convoy just west of Van Wert, including twenty-eight seasons as head coach of the Knights. In December, 2011, the school commemorated his career and service by naming their basketball facility the Ray Etzler Gymnasium.

The man many local basketball fans have long referred to as "King Richard" may never retire. Dick Kortokrax, as of this writing, is 80 years old and has been coaching basketball for nearly seventy-five percent of his life. While he had relatively brief stints at both Fort Jennings and Ottoville, when it comes to basketball, his name has become almost interchangeable with those schools' Putnam County neighbor, Kalida High School. He earned his Hall of Fame distinction in 1999, and, when his coaching days finally come to an end, will post a lifetime victory total (850 and counting) that may never be eclipsed in the state of Ohio.

The only female high school basketball coach from the area with a place in the Hall of Fame (Class of 2000) is Gretchen Prichard. She was at the forefront of molding girls' athletic programs at Bath in the early and mid-70's, and her impact went far beyond the tremendous success her teams enjoyed. The shear force of her personality inspired girls in elementary and middle school not only to look up to the older players in the Bath program but also to eagerly work to earn the right to follow in their footsteps by learning a sport's fundamentals as early as possible.

Three other men from this area entered the OHSBCA Hall of Fame in the first decade of the twenty-first century. Fran Guilbault's outstanding career at St. Henry earned him a place in the Class of 2001. Fran Voll's meteoric success in the early days of girls basketball at Delphos St. Johns in addition to his work as head women's coach at Bowling Green State University put him in the Class of 2003, and in 2008, the longtime boys coach at Ottawa-Glandorf, Dave Sweet, was inducted. In 26 years at the helm of the Titans, Sweet posted a record of 449-161 and won the Division II state title in 2004 with a dominant 33-point victory over Canal Fulton Northwest.

There are two more men on this area's OHSBCA Hall of Fame list, but first, I have some thoughts about coaches from the schools that made up the majority of my basketball broadcast schedule over the years.

If I were to list the local schools in the order of number of basketball games I broadcast for each, Lima Senior would be at the top of the page because that was the primary public school in my radio station's city of license. It is also interesting to note that Lima Senior had, by far, the largest number of boys' basketball coaches during my thirty-one year career.

Jim Romey was at the helm during my first broadcast season (1974-75) but stepped down after that campaign and passed away shortly thereafter. Those who knew him in his prime, however, have the utmost respect for Romey. Dave Cheney, the former Spartan standout who went on to play for the legendary Woody Hayes on one of the best college football teams of all time, the 1968 Ohio State national champions, remembers his line coach from his high school days, Romey, was without question the most versatile Lima Senior coach he ever experienced. He assisted Joe Bowers in baseball and Al Scrivner in football, for whom Cheney played. Recalls Cheney, "While Coach Romey probably is better known in Lima for basketball, he was a brilliant football coach and consummate motivator. He really is right in the conversation when it comes to the truly great coaches in Lima's history."

As for the Lima Senior basketball program, after Romey, eight other men guided the Spartans over the next three decades – Jim Robinson, who just recently entered the OHSBCA Hall of Fame in the class of 2014, Ron Niekamp, Jim Penn, Brad Ovial, Paul Whitney, Matt Creamer, Dick Heath and Mark Gaffney.

While I enjoyed good relationships with each of these coaches, the most memorable was Ron Niekamp. He played high school basketball for Fran Guilbault at St. Henry and then collegiately at Miami University in Oxford, Ohio. Upon graduation he coached basketball at Parkway High School for two years, then moved to Ottawa-Glandorf, where he led the Titans to the state tournament twice in five seasons.

Niekamp brought his talents to Lima in the late 70's and spent six years at Lima Senior. Led by high-flying 6'2" junior forward Bruce Andrews and a pair of senior guards, Steve Kimbrough and Eric Pitts, Niekamp's 1981-82 Spartans made it all the way to the Class AAA state semifinals before bowing to Cincinnati Roger Bacon 49-47 on a tip-in at the buzzer. That loss became even more painful the next day when Roger Bacon beat Barberton in the AAA championship game.

Two years later, an opportunity arose for Ron Niekamp to become head coach at the University of Findlay. There, he produced twenty-six straight winning seasons, and in 2008-09, had a season for the ages, as the Oilers forged a 36-0 mark and brought home to Flag City USA an NCAA Division II national championship. In his thirty-nine years as a head basketball coach at both the high school and college level, Niekamp's teams won 806 games and lost only 271, and he was so very appropriately inducted into the Ohio Basketball Hall of Fame in 2013.

While I have fond memories of several others, my boys basketball coaching mental catalogue at Bath, Shawnee and Elida centers on four key people.

Dwain Holt and Mark Shine guided the Bath program for most of my career. Their teams were consistently competitive against an always tough Western Buckeye League schedule, and both coaches were genuinely gracious people whose teams reflected their tenacity, intelligence and good sportsmanship. Perhaps drawing on his experience filling in for John Barton as my sidekick on the WIMA football broadcasts in 1996, Mark Shine continued his affiliation with high-school sports after retiring as a coach by working as a studio host and color commentator on WTLW-TV 44 in Lima.

When I think of Shawnee High School basketball, I think of Jeff Heistan. I first encountered Jeff in 1976 as a player at St. Marys Memorial High School in a tournament game at Ohio Northern when the Roughriders upset a heavily favored Delphos St. Johns team in the sectional finals. After playing four years at Heidelberg College, Jeff came to Lima as a varsity assistant at Lima Central Catholic for three years and then coached junior varsity for Jeff Johnides at Shawnee for four years.

In 1987, Heistan was named head boys coach at Shawnee and served in that role for the next seventeen years, taking the Indians to the state tournament in 2000. As the father of three daughters, Heistan also had a close affinity to the girls basketball program at Shawnee, and after stepping down as the boys coach in 2004, he coached the girls team for nine seasons, took one year off, and then returned as Shawnee's varsity girls basketball coach for the 2014-15 season.

The most famous player to come out of Shawnee during Heistan's tenure was Jamar Butler, the 2004 Associated Press's choice as Ohio's "Mr. Basketball." Butler went on to star while playing for Thad Matta at Ohio State. In one of the clearest examples of how basketball at any level is the consummate "team" sport, during Jamar's four years at Shawnee, the Indians never made it out of a sectional tournament while Lima's other two "Mr. Basketball" honorees, Greg Simpson and Aaron Hutchins, had good enough supporting casts to go all the way to the final four in Columbus during their careers at the two schools bearing Lima's name.

If my word association response to "Shawnee basketball" is Jeff Heistan, my immediate response to the words "Elida basketball" is Chris Adams. Although Chris was still in high school when I started at WIMA, he was the face of Bulldog basketball for the final twenty-one years of my career.

A native of Orrville, Ohio, Chris attended three different high schools in four years and played basketball each year before graduating from Lancaster in 1976. He played sparingly at Wittenberg University during his first two years there and then decided that learning to coach would be more productive than being a role player for two more seasons. So, he turned in his uniform and became a student-coach. After graduating from Wittenberg, Adams spent the next season as a full-time Wittenberg assistant coach before accepting his first head-coaching assignment at Springfield Catholic High School in 1981.

Four years later, the job at Elida opened up, and Chris Adams was selected to fill the position. The decision to give Adams the job translated to the Bulldogs' becoming solid WBL contenders every year for the next two decades. His arrival at Elida coincided with the demise of the old Lima Holiday Tournament, which featured Lima Senior, Lima Central Catholic, Shawnee and Bath. Adams wasted no time suggesting the Elida Tip-Off Classic as a way to begin the basketball season for Elida, Shawnee, Bath and LCC. It is a much anticipated event that continues to this day.

Chris realized that media coverage of high school sports in Northwest Ohio was unlike anything he had seen in the state's bigger cities and was quick to take advantage of every opportunity afforded him to promote Elida basketball. "I always thought that one of my jobs as a head coach was to promote my players in any way possible," he told me, "to maybe further their chances in using basketball as a way to get to the collegiate level or to just better themselves in general." Among his many talents as both coach and promoter, Chris possessed the instinctive ability to answer a reporter's questions in succinct but meaningful ways that were perfect for the fifteen-to-twenty second sound bites necessary for radio or television use.

To watch Chris Adams coach a high school game was akin to watching a human version of the Energizer Bunny in action. Equal

measures of intensity, enthusiasm, sideline pacing, an occasional
outburst of temper and his ability to produce a fundamentally
sound basketball team created a recipe that local fans will
remember for a long time.

Although Elida's two most heralded players, Reggie
McAdams (Akron) and Dustin Mathias (Purdue), played for the
Bulldogs and earned Division I basketball scholarships after Coach
Adams retired in 2005, he sent several players to the college ranks
during his career as well, including Mark Bishop, Jon Woolley,
Matt Metzger and his son, Drew Adams.

Upon his retirement from high-school coaching, Adams
was hired as athletic director and men's basketball coach at the
University of Northwestern Ohio in Lima and has overseen a
program that has joined the NAIA's Wolverine-Hoosier Athletic
Conference and grown from just volleyball and basketball at
the beginning to thirteen varsity sports and four junior-varsity
programs in less than ten years.

The only local high school basketball coach with more time
on the bench than Chris Adams while I worked at WIMA is Lima
Central Catholic's Bob Seggerson, whose universal moniker in this
part of Ohio is simply "Segg."

Segg was born in Lima, grew up amongst eight siblings,
seven of whom were brothers, played football and basketball at
Lima Central Catholic from 1962 to 1966 and then competed on
the hardwood at St. Joseph's College in Indiana for four years. He
came back to Lima after college in 1970 and returned to his high-
school alma mater. For the first few years, Segg coached cross
country and girls tennis in addition to being an assistant in football
and basketball. He then succeeded Jim Carder as head basketball
coach at LCC in 1978 and spent the next thirty-two years in that
role while also serving as a guidance counselor to countless LCC
students.

While Segg's record of 510 wins and 209 losses, six trips
to the state tournament, and one Division III state title in his final
year as a head coach (2010) are impressive enough, when you add
the fact that for the first twenty-five years of his career, LCC did

not play in a conference and did not have a home court, his record becomes even more remarkable.

Until a brand new gym opened at LCC in 2003, the Thunderbirds shared Lima Senior's gymnasium for boys basketball. That meant that the T-Birds rarely played a Friday night game for two reasons. First, the Spartans always had a conference schedule to satisfy and had priority usage of the gym and second, virtually every LCC opponent played in a conference and, therefore, was not available to play on most Friday nights.

Since LCC's basketball schedule involved primarily Tuesday and Saturday night games, Segg's Friday nights were spent scouting. He told me that he rarely stayed beyond the middle of the third quarter, however, so he could get in his car to drive home and immediately turn on WIMA radio to listen to our broadcast.

I was humbled by something he was so very kind to say to me as he reflected on his time carving his own coaching legacy. "I would flip from station to station to check on as many as six or seven other games, but I didn't think any of them had the professionalism or the insights I was getting from WIMA, so I would listen to whatever game was on, even if it involved teams that we would never play that year."

My snapshot photo of Bob Seggerson on any game night in any season will always remain ingrained in my memory. That image is of a tall, slender man in khaki pants with a long-sleeved blue Oxford shirt and a tie that's not fully cinched to the unbuttoned neckline. Influenced by the likes of Bobby Knight and Al McGuire, Segg was primarily a defensive coach who instilled a system that his players could implement regardless of the game circumstance. In his words, "I would simply say this is what we do when 'x' happens and do it. And it worked."

Segg suffered more heartache as a head coach than any man with whom I ever worked, losing five state tournament games by a total of just eight points, but he never let those disappointments define him, his team or his school. When the infamous call against Salento Boddie in 1992 allowed Berlin Hiland to make three free throws in the final second and pull off their miracle 64-62

comeback win in the state semifinals, Segg made a decision not
to make a big deal about the official's call although he knew that
would be the focus of the post-game press conference. "I didn't
want LCC's program to be associated with sour grapes," he
told me, "and I'm glad I made that decision." In such a difficult
moment, right after the heat of battle, how laudatory it was that
Seggerson would place the reputation of the school before his own
extreme disappointment.

One of my biggest disappointments as a broadcaster was
being retired and, therefore, not behind the WIMA microphone
to call Segg's state championship triumph over Orrville in 2010.
No one was ever more deserving of such a final career game, and
the ink was barely dry on Segg's retirement papers before the
OHSBCA voted him into the 2011 class of their Hall of Fame.

As close as I was to coaches like Chris Adams and Bob
Seggerson during my time at WIMA, I had no idea that our paths
would cross again as the three of us entered the post-high school
phase of our lives. Before delving into how the three of us have
remained somewhat intertwined, there are some other hallmark
memories of my days in the WIMA studios at 667 W. Market
Street in Lima that deserve some air time.

Other WIMA Highlights

While most people in this area associate me with my primary workplace passion, the play-by-play portion of my broadcasting career, I also experienced a great deal of satisfaction from other aspects of the industry during a time in history when radio was the primary electronic source for news, weather, sports and musical entertainment.

WIMA dominated the listenership numbers for so many years because station management made a concerted effort to assemble a team of seasoned professionals both on the air and behind the scenes. We considered ourselves a family, and each employee knew that his or her contribution to the broadcast product was both needed and very much appreciated. Additionally, the staff believed that the public-service role of the station was as important as the daily programming content, and that was never more evident than during the worst weather-related event in my four decades in this community.

When most people went to bed on Thursday, January 26, 1978, some overnight snow was predicted, but temperatures were a couple of degrees above freezing and there was no sense of immediate urgency. However, just after midnight, a large trough of warm moist air from the south began to collide with a strong arctic cold front over much of the state.

The system produced approximately 70 MPH winds, heavy snow and temperatures that plummeted into single digits. Additionally, the lowest barometric pressure reading (28.28 inches of mercury) in Ohio history was recorded. And, what did such a confluence of weather-related occurrences produce? By the time Ohioans awoke on Friday and looked out their windows, they saw a landscape that in so many ways resembled the Klondike.

By the time the storm ended, the amount of actual snowfall in this area measured between 20 and 30 inches, but the strong winds had produced drifts that ranged from three or four feet to as high as twenty-five feet in some places. Two-lane roads were completely impassable, especially in the rural areas, and only the sturdiest four-wheel drive vehicles could negotiate the major thoroughfares. By daybreak on Friday, the entire listening area was at a virtual standstill.

Almost immediately, WIMA radio became one of the only dependable links to information about the natural disaster. Personal computers and cell phones did not yet exist, and sporadic power outages meant that many landline telephones were inoperable. People scrambled to find batteries because transistor radios were the only way for the public to receive messages from city and county emergency officials.

I was still living at 1500 West High Street, about ten blocks away from the WIMA studios and remember our maintenance man, Ernie Cottman, picking me up early that Friday morning and driving me to the station in a four-wheel drive vehicle over the one lane that somehow had been kept passable on West Market Street. Similar efforts were made to assemble other key WIMA staff members, and for the next three to four days, our studios became a community-information command center.

The National Guard brought Army cots so that our air personalities and news people could rest between live shifts. Generous listeners with snowmobiles dropped off food and drink.

Power to our radio station went down early in the storm, but an emergency generator kept WIMA on the air until power crews could get the grid for our block of West Market Street back on line. Although radio in the late '70s was primarily associated with entertainment, especially playing music, during this most challenging time, we didn't play a single musical selection for three days.

Our around-the-clock programming consisted of passing along every form of emergency information imaginable as well as being a link for school, plant and business closings; shelter locations for those without power; and even airing an occasional need for a volunteer snowmobiler to deliver essential medications to someone unable to leave their home.

By the end of the weekend, although schools would stay closed for the next full week, major area roads were passable enough that if a person could get the huge drifts out of his own driveway, he could make it to a grocery store, and finally the WIMA staff was able to relax a bit and get back to a regular work schedule. As grueling as that experience was, I was never as proud of my workplace as the time we provided an electronic lifeline to the entire listening area during what, for residents of Northwest Ohio old enough to remember, will always be known as "The Blizzard of '78."

One endearing memory of the event occurred while I was manning the front-desk phone lines on the Monday morning after the blizzard. I answered a call from a lady who asked if I could help her with a special concern. I could tell from the sound of her voice that she was elderly and a bit agitated, so I calmly said, "If there's any way I can help you, I will."

Her next words were, "I haven't received my *Lima News* for three days now. Is there any way you could read the obituaries over the air?" Having not yet reached the age where a glance at the obits was one of the first parts of my daily ritual, and, given the fact that we didn't have so much as a fax machine yet at our front desk, I chuckled a bit to myself before politely replying, "I'm sorry but we haven't received a newspaper here at the station either since the blizzard started, so I can't fulfill your request because, like you, we don't know who has passed away over the last three days." This episode confirms the reality that everyone's priorities are different during a time of crisis.

Until WIMA was sold by Lima Broadcasting Company to Clear Channel in 1999, local personalities filled the radio day from 6 AM until midnight, and a well-staffed news department kept the public apprised of happenings within the community. In addition to five-minute newscasts at the top and bottom of each hour, there was a full hour of news, weather, sports and farm market information along with Paul Harvey from noon until 1 PM each weekday.

Those driving home between five and six in the evening or listening while preparing dinner heard a program called "Sixty Till Six," which was similar to the noon news block but also contained the closing market information on stocks of local interest as well as the closing farm commodity prices for the day.

It was also this evening news block that gave me the opportunity to expand my sports coverage. In addition to a five-minute segment of straight sports news, I lobbied for and was given an additional three-minute slot during the hour for "Mullen It Over." I chose that name for the feature because it was the title I had used for the column I wrote in high school for the Gonzaga student newspaper, and, of course, because my last name sounded so similar to the phrase "mulling it over." It really fit the segment well.

On some days, "Mullen It Over" was simply an explanation of upcoming athletic events such as giving the pairings for basketball tournament games that were scheduled in the area that evening and highlighting those with the most local interest. On other days, I featured an in-depth taped interview with an area sports personality. But I most appreciated this platform because it gave me a regular opportunity to editorialize on topics that were of interest to all levels of sports fans.

Rarely a day went by without an item coming up in sports that I felt needed more explanation or background for the average fan to understand it than a fifteen-second sound bite could impart. Since the "Sixty Till Six" audience included a wide age range and level of sports interest, I tried to focus on discussing sports-related topics in terms that a person who'd never listened to a game or knew what a box score was could understand.

From the early 1980's until the late 1990's, I'm both thankful and proud to say that "Mullen It Over" found an audience, and our numbers revealed that the segment became one of WIMA's most popular broadcast products. In fact, when I was out in public and introduced to someone I didn't know, instead of receiving a routine "Nice to meet you" with a handshake, I often experienced a first reaction such as, "Oh, so you're 'Mullen It Over'!"

When Clear Channel took over ownership of the Lima Broadcasting Company properties in 1999, programming changes were not far behind. Music formats on AM radio stations were being phased out because they could not compete with the quality of stereo FM stations or the growing tendency of people to listen to tapes or CD music on portable electronic devices. Clear Channel also had contracts with major talk show hosts like Rush Limbaugh, Glenn Beck, Sean Hannity and others; and it became much cheaper for my new bosses to replace local air talents with these nationally syndicated shows.

Before long, WIMA radio took on a completely new look. Its longtime recipe of disc jockeys playing music was replaced with a talk-radio format. With the exception of a live local personality from 6 AM to 9 AM, WIMA turned into a steady stream of syndicated news or sports talk shows. While the station still carried a full schedule of Reds, Bengals, Ohio State and local game broadcasts, the news department was scaled back and lengthy local news blocks with features like "Mullen It Over" were eliminated.

Another transition that affected my job significantly was the change from the era of turntables and eight-track cartridges to computers and the whole world of digital technology. While the result was much easier and actually produced a better quality of audio for our broadcasts, the transition resembled the old adage about sausage, as in, it's great but you don't want to watch how they make it.

During the spring of 1989, station management was aware of the inroads that computers were making in the radio industry and tasked our two engineers, Mark Gierhart and Dick Knowles, with designing a method by which computers rather than people could reliably generate the music and commercials that were the mainstays of our airwaves. The immediate goal was to automate both WIMA and our sister station, T-102 on FM, from midnight to 6 AM, but the long-term vision was to eventually bring all station functions into the digital age.

At the time, I didn't even own a personal computer and had absolutely no knowledge of how to use one. Our air personalities played music from records on a turntable, and those staff members charged with producing commercials either read them live during their air shift or recorded them on eight-track cartridges commonly referred to as carts.

For pre-recorded commercials on carts, we used a system. When a client placed an order to air his commercials, we assigned a cart number for the programming that he was sponsoring. When we produced the client's commercials, we recorded them on a cart that was then labeled with the business's name and cart number. We then placed the carts in a rack in the studio control room so that we could play them when they appeared on the broadcast log.

When I did a local high school ballgame, for example, the board operator pulled the carts from the studio storage rack in the order in which the game log called for them to be aired. At each time out, he played the number of commercials I needed and then replaced the carts in their numerical sequence in the storage rack.

The process was simple and worked very smoothly for more than two decades until the computers suddenly arrived in the time it took to get a weekend's worth of good sleep, and technology most assuredly took over our broadcast lives. I went home one Friday afternoon in the fall of 1989 with turntables and cart machines resting comfortably in their assigned locations, much like friends you temporarily take leave of before seeing again, and returned on Monday morning at 5 AM to find the studio looking like a movie set from *Star Trek* without any of my old friends in sight. Our engineering tag-team of Gierhart and Knowles had accomplished their assigned task.

Without as much as a minute's worth of training, the morning crew was told to do the best we could and, in effect, learn this whole computer thing on the fly. It was explained to us that the only way to enter the digital world was to use the same strategy employed by those entering a chilly swimming pool. You don't get wet inch by inch. Rather, you just have to dive in all at once and deal with it.

The turntables, record bins, cart machines and cart storage racks were all gone. The music, commercials and public-service spots, basically everything we had to have was in the computer. Suffice it to say that for the next few weeks, listening to WIMA radio was like watching people at a Bob Evans factory make sausage. It was messy and probably, for our listeners, not very enjoyable.

As computers became more a part of our working environment, advances in radio station operating systems came along every couple of years. And, while these were often advertised as "easier and more efficient," they often turned out to be "complicated and more time consuming." One new system called, for some totally inexplicable reason, "Prophet" came along in the mid-90's and brought challenges I never expected as a sportscaster.

While game logs had been prepared in the past showing the order of commercials to be run and the board operator simply wrote the time each spot aired on the log for future billing purposes, the new "Prophet" system required that each commercial be given a specific hour-and-minute air time in advance so that it would automatically be played and subsequently billed. Given the nature of high school ballgames, I immediately knew that this arrangement wouldn't work.

I approached the transition person the computer company had furnished to help us learn the new operating system and told her the format was in no way compatible with a local high school broadcast. She was a young woman who had experience programming a professional basketball radio network in California and thought all games had pre-determined starting times and commercial breaks. She said the computer program for local ballgames on WIMA was based on that model.

I informed her that high school ballgames did not have pre-planned media time outs and that I had no control over when the in-game commercials might be needed. Additionally, she had no idea that junior varsity games preceded our varsity broadcasts, so air time each evening was totally dependent on what time the JV game ended and could not be pre-determined. I finished what must have been a disheartening list of problems by explaining that if we were to honor our commitment to air a client's commercials during game broadcasts, and ultimately get paid for those spots, she would have to change the computer program.

After some initial resistance on her part, we were able to develop a viable solution, but from that day forward, a pre-game process to check to see if all the commercials were there that used to take me five minutes at most during the previous twenty years took at least thirty minutes, thanks to the wonderful efficiency of our new "Prophet" computer operating system.

Mixed in among the thousands of sportscasts, game broadcasts and advertising sales efforts that dotted my career was an annual event that was dedicated to showcasing the best student-athletes in the area. It's an event that I count as one of my biggest blessings, the opportunity to play a significant role in recognizing those on whom I relied for a career I found so very fulfilling.

On May 21, 1975, the Lima Area Chamber of Commerce hosted the first high school sports awards banquet in the city. The business leaders in the community wanted to recognize top seniors from the six high schools in Lima. Since organized sports for girls had barely emerged on the high school level, only male seniors nominated by their schools from the sports of football, basketball, wrestling, track and baseball came to this inaugural event.

As the brand new sports director at WIMA, I was invited to be on the Chamber of Commerce panel that would select the top player in each sport from the schools' nominees. All thirty nominees, their parents and also their coaches were invited to a special dinner at the Milano Club, Lima's acknowledged top local Italian restaurant, then located on West Market Street in downtown Lima. At the banquet, all players were introduced and recognized, but only the top player in each sport, as picked by the selection panel, was given a commemorative plaque.

The first guest speaker at the 1975 sports banquet was longtime Dayton television sports anchor, Omar Williams. The evening went well, and as often happens in these types of events, the concept of recognizing our local athletes gained momentum over the next several years. Because the Chamber of Commerce was behind it and because it was during an era where prominent coaches would willingly consent to sports-related speaking engagements without financial remuneration, honorees at the next five sports awards banquets heard from several nationally known figures, such as Woody Hayes, Forrest Gregg, Eldon Miller, Archie Griffin and Sparky Anderson.

Eventually, the banquet expanded to include girls basketball and volleyball nominees, and each year I remained part of the selection committee to choose the overall winner in each sport. Gradually, however, the idea of choosing one person out of six in each sport to receive a plaque began to produce negative rumblings from the schools' officials because they, and justifiably so, felt it was too difficult to establish a consistent selection criteria.

For example, how do you compare a running back in football with a defensive end, given the fact that assessing each player's performance is so vastly different? Is a point guard who averages 18 points per game better than a center who averages 11 points a game but is a great rebounder and shot blocker? How do you say a sprinter is a better track athlete than the guy who throws the discus? The discord finally reached a point where some schools were becoming reluctant to nominate athletes for the banquet.

About eight years into the project, a couple of us on the selection committee proposed that the Chamber of Commerce do away with the concept that there be a big plaque for the overall winner and simply give smaller plaques to every nominee in each sport. A slightly bigger budget would be necessary, but it would result in equal acclamation for all the athletes and eliminate any chance of hurt feelings or ill will on the part of the schools or the general public.

That recommendation was adopted, and the banquet continued to grow each year as more boys and girls sports were added. After the thirteenth annual event in 1987, the Chamber of Commerce decided that the banquet was becoming too large for it to support and was going to end its sponsorship. I had been associated with each one to that point and certainly didn't want to see the tradition end.

So, I went to my boss at WIMA, Les Rau, and told him about the impending fate of the sports banquet. I thought it would be an excellent opportunity for WIMA to step in as the major sponsor and, perhaps, even broaden the scope of the event. Mr. Rau agreed, on the condition that I would personally organize the banquet and solicit other underwriting sponsors to help offset the overall cost. I agreed, and from 1988 until I retired in 2005, it was a project that kept me busy from the end of basketball season through late May each year.

During my first year as the coordinator and emcee, I made few changes, but after the 1988 banquet I enlisted the help of the WIMA sales team in order to secure several other underwriters. Additional sponsors were necessary because a big expansion was in the works. In 1989 we took the wraps off an event we dubbed the Allen County High School Sports Awards Banquet and invited top senior athletes from the major sports at all twelve high schools in the county. That expansion also required moving the venue from the Milano Club to the Veterans' Memorial Civic and Convention Center in downtown Lima in order to accommodate the additional athletes, coaches and parents.

One year later, in 1990, Mr. Rau approved the final banquet expansion, enabling us to include top male and female senior athletes in all sports at all twelve schools. Forty years later, the event that began rather humbly one night in May of 1975 when thirty boys were honored at the town's first high school sports awards banquet has grown by leaps and bounds. The Civic Center now routinely welcomes between five and six hundred people for a sit-down dinner on banquet night. That group includes 150-160 athletes (depending on the year and whether a school has seniors participating in all sports), their coaches, and their parents and family.

Over the years, the major sponsors have underwritten the rental cost of the venue and the meal costs for all the athletes and their head coaches. Family members and other school officials are charged only for the cost of their meals. The event has also triggered in-kind donations of items such as the plaques, the program printing costs, and soft drinks for each table.

As time progressed, it became more difficult to secure speakers with the pedigree of, say, a Woody Hayes or a Sparky Anderson, because modern occupants of such positions either work through agents who demand large speaking fees no matter what the circumstance, or, frankly, have so many demands on their time and make so much money that they don't even consider such requests.

Nevertheless, in 1992, Ohio State basketball coach Randy Ayers agreed to speak because Lima Senior's Greg Simpson had signed to play that fall for the Buckeyes. In 1994, local coaching legend Bob Arnzen was the keynote speaker. The Commissioner of the Ohio High School Athletic Association, Clair Muscaro, spoke in 1997, and speakers with names like Ohio State Athletic Director Andy Geiger, then Bowling Green basketball coach Dan Dakich and also BG's football coach at that time, Urban Meyer, would follow.

I chose the 2005 Allen County High School Sports Awards Banquet as the place publicly to announce my impending retirement from WIMA Radio, and I was doubly honored that evening to have the assembled group of high school seniors be addressed by a man who sat in their place in 1986, my son, Jeff Mullen, who played both football and baseball at Lima Senior.

By 2005, Jeff had been a Division I football coach for fourteen years following his collegiate playing days at Wittenberg

University and was the quarterbacks coach on Jim Grobe's staff at Wake Forest University.

With my family in attendance and with my son delivering the keynote address and the immense pride I felt watching the kind of man my boy had become, I was content in the knowledge that after 31 straight years of watching top high school senior student-athletes honored for their hard work and success, I would be handing the sports awards banquet gavel over to the man who would succeed me at WIMA, Todd Walker.

Although I publicly announced my intention to leave WIMA on that banquet night in May of 2005, I did not intend to end my relationship with the station officially until the end of November that year. And while I had no specific retirement plans, I was not concerned because I have always believed that such details work out in due time and according to the Lord's plan.

So, as I reflected on the many facets of my more than three decades in Lima, I eagerly looked forward to the process of first discovering and then meeting new challenges.

My Second Career

In retrospect, my time has gone by quickly, in large part because I was lucky enough to discover my passion and find a way to make it my life's work. From the day I accepted Chuck Osburn's offer to do weekend sports at WLIO-TV to the final time I set my alarm clock at 4:45 AM to ensure getting to WIMA in time for the morning show, I can say I'm proud of what I did and how I did it.

In addition to a book's worth of experiences in the sports world, including a two-year term in 1981-82 as president of the Ohio Sportscasters Association, I was also blessed to be a part of several volunteer projects designed to give something back to the community I grew to embrace as my own.

During my early years in Lima, following the lead of my TV boss, I helped promote and facilitate the American Cancer Society's "Swim-A-Long" fundraiser each summer. Local and area youth swim clubs took part and helped raise money to fight cancer by securing pledges from friends and family for swimming laps during their summer workouts.

My barber of four decades, Dick Smallwood, was a master at recruiting enthusiastic people with a variety of skills and business connections and blending those talents and material donations into meaningful renovations to the city's high school football site. I was more than happy to lend my support to his efforts, especially during the addition of new lights and the construction of a new two-story press box at the original Lima Stadium in the late '80s.

In 1982, I joined a local service organization known as the Lima Exchange Club and have continued as a member to this day. Exchange Clubs throughout America have chosen Child Abuse Prevention as their main focus. I have been active on the board several times and twice served as the club's president. I'm very proud of the work our members do throughout the year to assist those who work tirelessly in agencies in Lima and Allen County to help reduce child abuse in our community.

Through my association with the Exchange Club, I met David Voth, who heads an agency in Lima called Crime Victims Services. David and his staff do an outstanding job of ensuring that victims of crime are properly helped as they navigate through the often-daunting criminal justice system.

When David asked me to join the agency's board of directors, I gladly accepted and served from 1995 through 2001, including one term as board president.

As the twenty-first century dawned and the computer scare Y2K came and went without a hint of predicted digital chaos, the idea of retiring began to appear on my horizon. I thought and prayed a lot about the matter and eventually settled on a personal formula to help guide me as to when to make that choice. I told myself that if there ever came a time when I was sitting at my kitchen table late on a Friday afternoon eating a pre-game sandwich and saying to myself, "Damn, I have another game to broadcast tonight," it was time to step down.

On several Friday afternoons during the 2004-05 basketball season, that kitchen-table scenario became a reality, so I began seriously to contemplate leaving WIMA. I would turn 62 in October of 2005 and, therefore, be eligible to start drawing Social Security. Additionally, I figured that even if my generally good health continued, I could expect about fifteen more years of having the strength, interest, and mobility to travel and to see my grandkids grow up, and I wanted to savor as much of that time as possible. My retirement plan was officially in motion.

As I sat at courtside on the final Saturday night of the 2005 boys state basketball tournament in Columbus, it was somehow fitting that my last high school broadcast featured a Canton McKinley win over Cincinnati St. Xavier 51-42 in the Division I championship game. Thirty years earlier, with John Barton at my side, McKinley's loss in the state semifinals triggered the fan eruption and on-air epithet that had me worried about FCC sanctions. Now, with George Frazee in the chair beside me, the jubilant Bulldog fans were celebrating their second championship in school history and happy to let me do my final post-game show in peace.

Although I would not officially retire until November 30, 2005, I knew in March of that year that my high school play-by-play days were over. I was fortunate that my successor, Todd Walker, was already in place. Todd had been a member of our radio staff for more than ten years and was fully capable of handling any on-air assignment.

Early in his career, the former Allen East football and basketball standout was an air personality on WIMA's sister station, WBUK. Additionally, he was both comfortable and entertaining as a fill-in talk show host, handled the daily sportscast duties when I was on vacation, and had several years of play-by-play experience as well working girls basketball broadcasts and occasional boys tournament games when we covered multiple contests from different sites on the same night. Given Todd's experience and talent, I was confident that his transition to sports director would be seamless for both himself and the listening audience.

While I was ready to retire and, frankly, happy to give up a work schedule chock full of very early mornings and, sometimes, quite late evenings, my wife, Amy, continued her full-time employment with the Ohio Bureau of Workers' Compensation in Lima. She enjoyed her work as an employer service specialist, and her income and family insurance coverage was an essential part of our financial game plan.

Once the Christmas holiday season passed and the calendar turned to 2006, I began to focus on finding something to do on a part-time basis, and it wasn't long before my prayers and patience paid off when not one but two opportunities presented themselves.

In late 2005, a man named Don Bachman passed away after an extended illness. Don was a longtime high school sports official from Van Wert, Ohio, and had served as the Commissioner of the Northwest Conference (NWC) for more than thirty years. At the time, the NWC was a ten-school athletic conference that included Ada, Allen East, Bluffton, Columbus Grove, Crestview, Delphos Jefferson, Lincolnview, Paulding, Spencerville and Upper Scioto Valley.

An athletic conference commissioner at the high school level has two primary duties – to assign officials for varsity conference games in several sports and to act as the recording secretary for all conference meetings of principals and athletic directors. The job of NWC president rotated each year amongst the principals of the participating schools. During the 2005-06 school year, that position was filled by Bluffton High School principal, Greg Deneker.

Early in 2006, I learned that, because of the passing of Don Bachman, the NWC was looking for a new commissioner. Since the position involved working with many people I already knew in the high school sports world, I thought it might be a logical career segue, so I took steps to find out exactly what the job entailed, how much it paid and how much time it would require.

Once I had that information and knew that the job demands would fit comfortably into my retirement schedule, I sent a letter to Mr. Deneker and formally applied for the position. Two other area officials also applied, including Don Bachman's son, Randy, and another Van Wert official, Ron Golemon. Together they had been doing most of the commissioner's work for Randy's failing father during the months prior to his passing.

When I appeared before the committee of NWC principals assigned to interview the commissioner candidates, I focused on two attributes that I believed would be of value to the NWC. First, I was a well-respected veteran of more than thirty years in sports broadcasting and was familiar with generating press releases which, because of my media connections, would help ensure area-wide coverage of NWC activities. Second, I had never been a certified official in any sport, so I offered something in which the conference had a growing interest, complete neutrality when it came to assigning officials.

As I researched the potential position, I became aware that a number of qualified area officials had concerns about the NWC. Apparently, during the latter years of his tenure as commissioner, Mr. Bachman had been prone to hire the same veteran circle of officiating friends for key conference games. If other officials did secure NWC contracts, they were generally assigned to the least competitive matchups. This trend had also been noticed by some athletic directors in the NWC, thereby prompting their interest in finding a commissioner who would draw officials both from a larger geographic area and from a broader age demographic.

In March, 2006, I received a call from Mr. Deneker informing me that the conference principals had selected me as their new commissioner. Since officials for NWC baseball and softball games in the spring of 2006 had long since been assigned, I was told I would officially start my new position on July 1. That gave me three months to gather the files on officials who had already been contracted for the 2006-07 school year and beyond, and, hopefully, to get some pointers from Randy Bachman on how to best fill the commissioner's role.

Unfortunately, I never received the first bit of help from Randy. When he was not chosen to follow in his father's footsteps, instead of helping me with the transition, he tendered his immediate resignation as acting commissioner, boxed up the conference files, and dropped them off at Bluffton High School without a word of comment or explanation. All of a sudden I became the NWC commissioner three months before my expected start date.

The athletic director at Bluffton High School, Jim Raabe,

proved to be a lifesaver over the next few months. He generously helped me sift through the loosely organized files, and together we did our best to determine which officials had been hired for the next year's volleyball, football, basketball, baseball and softball seasons and which games they had been assigned.

Suffice it to say the previous NWC commissioner's strong point was not attention to detail. As the 2006-07 school year unfolded, there were several instances where two football crews instead of one, or six varsity basketball officials instead of three, or four umpires instead of two showed up for a conference game. This happened because, without benefit of a transition period with my predecessor, I had no choice but to hire officials for all contests that did not show evidence of signed contracts. For some of those games, however, it turned out that the previous commissioner had secured officials but had not documented those hires in the conference file.

Now, OHSAA guidelines for assigners require that the earliest-dated contracts in such situations be honored, and that both sets of officials be paid if the discrepancy occurs without sufficient time for the double-booked officials to find other assignments on the dates in question. There were a couple occasions where I learned of a double-booking far enough in advance to secure other assignments for everyone involved, but several times the NWC had to absorb the cost of paying extra officials who didn't work because of the scheduling snafu. By the 2007-08 school year, I had resolved any similar issues far enough in advance that things ran smoothly from that point on.

From the spring of 2006, I served as NWC Commissioner for the next seven years. I enjoyed the opportunity to remain involved in high school athletics and weathered the technological change in the process of hiring officials from paper contracts sent via regular mail to electronic contracts done completely on-line. The only controversy during my seven years as commissioner involved the coming and going of Lima Central Catholic as a conference member.

As for the first chapter of the LCC-NWC saga, the story

began in 2004 when Upper Scioto Valley High School, citing
an insufficient number of players, abruptly cancelled its football
program, leaving many NWC opponents scrambling to find a
replacement game for that season. Going forward, USV wanted to
stay in the conference in all sports except football, but the other
NWC schools were not in favor of that arrangement. Since that
option wasn't available, USV ultimately withdrew from the NWC
and joined a newly formed group of smaller schools called the
Northwest Central Conference (NWCC).

With the NWC down to nine members, Lima Central
Catholic applied to join the conference, a request the Thunderbirds
had made once before a number of years earlier without success.
After months of considerable debate, a majority of NWC principals
approved LCC's request in March of 2006, despite the reservations
of at least three of the nine schools, and granted the Thunderbirds
membership starting with the 2006-07 school year.

The reservations of the dissenting NWC school
administrators centered around the fact that LCC had a talented
student athletic pool in place at the time of their request for
admission. Additionally, the dissenters felt that since LCC
was a parochial school which, under OHSAA guidelines, was
permitted to draw students from anywhere in Allen County, there
was somewhat of a disadvantage for public schools, which were
restricted to student-athletes living in their own school districts.

This OHSAA-approved broader area of geographical drawing
power for parochial schools is common throughout Ohio, and, in
my opinion, also logical because there are roughly four times as
many public schools in the state with clearly defined albeit smaller
school-district boundaries. The disparity of sizes between parochial
and public school districts has, over time, created an undercurrent
of perception among many high school sports fans that the Catholic
schools "recruit" some athletes because they don't have the same
limited district boundaries as the public schools. It is my belief that
vestiges of this sentiment also played into the misgivings of some
NWC schools about bringing LCC into the fold.

So, about the same time I was hired as the new NWC

commissioner, I also learned that LCC would be its newest
member. Despite the misgivings I have cited, I considered it to be
a win-win for both parties. I believed that athletic-performance
levels within the conference would gradually improve because of
LCC's arrival, and having a Lima school in the conference would
mean more media coverage for all NWC teams. As for the other
win, with its nearly thirty-year stretch as an athletic independent
now over, LCC's student-athletes would enjoy the benefits of
playing for honors such as NWC titles and recognition on all-
conference teams.

From the beginning, and to the surprise of very few,
LCC's overall athletic strength dominated conference play. The
Thunderbirds won the Don Bachman Award, the conference's all-
sports trophy named for the previous NWC commissioner, their
first four years in the conference and six times in seven years.
The Thunderbirds were particularly dominant in the two sports
that generated the most community fan interest and conversation,
football and boys basketball.

My experience as a high school broadcaster tells me that
most high school fans don't pay much attention to which team
wins the conference title in golf or softball, but if the general
perception is that their school has little or no chance to compete
for a championship in football or boys basketball because of a
conference newcomer, fans get a bit surly and start putting pressure
on administrators to do something about it.

In my opinion, this is what happened in the school districts
that weren't in favor of accepting LCC in the first place. Given the
Thunderbirds' early overall athletic success, and following a 2011
football campaign which included a perfect 10-0 regular-season
record and LCC's fourth conference title in six years, the pressure
in some communities that had been simmering since 2006 came to
a boil. In a matter of days a coalition of school administrators who
wanted the NWC to go back to the way it was before LCC was
admitted quietly made their thoughts known to their peers, hoping
to generate enough support to oust the Thunderbirds.

The coalition faced a problem, however, because LCC was

a conference member in good standing and there was no way to vote them out within the existing NWC bylaws. Naturally, LCC athletic director Ron Williams was aware of the growing unrest. He knew that the Thunderbirds could legally stand their ground in the NWC, but after conferring with his school's administration, the decision was made to be proactive and diffuse any further discord. The school did not want LCC athletes and coaches to be forced to compete long term in such an awkward conference environment.

And so it was that on December 1, 2011, Mr. Williams submitted a letter announcing that Lima Central Catholic was formally withdrawing from the Northwest Conference effective June 30, 2013. On the surface, it looked like a hasty and perhaps unnecessary capitulation to some disgruntled fans in a couple of conference school districts, but, in my opinion, it was a principled and courageous athletic director and school administration taking the high road in order to avoid a situation that would have only grown more rancorous over time.

The news of LCC's departure from the NWC came as quite a surprise to area sports fans because the whole matter, from the flare up to the ultimate resolution, took barely three weeks and not even a whisper of it had surfaced in the local media. LCC's willingness voluntarily to withdraw from the NWC was contingent upon a departure date that was eighteen months away. LCC was essentially saying, "We'll leave peacefully if you give us a workable exit strategy that will allow both us and the other conference schools adequate time to adjust our athletic schedules." LCC's letter of withdrawal succeeded in quieting those who were looking for an even quicker removal of the Thunderbirds and was formally accepted by the conference.

When I applied for the NWC commissioner's job in 2006, I told the interview panel that I was willing to commit to at least five years in office but couldn't promise anything beyond that. I was five and a half years into the position when the move to oust LCC reared its head.

During the last couple of weeks of November, 2011, I lost some of the respect I had for certain conference administrators over the way the LCC issue had been handled, so after careful consideration, and knowing that I wanted more time to be able to watch the activities of my grandkids who were reaching middle and high-school age, I decided to retire after seven years as NWC commissioner on June 30, 2013, the date that coincided with the end of LCC's seven-year stay. I was very capably succeeded by the man who helped me get started in the job, the now-retired athletic director from Bluffton High School, Jim Raabe.

A bit earlier I mentioned that not one but two opportunities for part-time retirement work presented themselves just months after I left WIMA. Shortly after I began my tenure as the NWC commissioner, my long-time friend Chris Adams called one day in early June and asked me to have lunch with him. He hinted that he had an idea he wanted me to consider, so I gladly accepted his invitation.

I knew that Chris had retired as a teacher and head boys basketball coach at Elida at the end of the 2005-06 school year. What I didn't know until we met for lunch was that he had accepted a job offer from the University of Northwestern Ohio (UNOH) in Lima and that this local institution of higher learning which had not fielded organized athletic teams in nearly thirty years was about to get back into that extra-curricular field in a big way.

UNOH traces its roots to a downtown Lima office building in 1920 where it started as Northwestern Business College. In 1973, the school needed more space so it moved to Cable Road on the west side of Lima, where it added what would become nationally recognized programs in auto-diesel mechanics and heating, ventilation and cooling (HVAC) training.

With both a business college and a technical school now in place, the school changed its name and became known as NBC Tech, which was short for Northwestern Business College - Technical Center. Over the next forty years, the campus and school name evolved into the now flourishing and fully accredited University of Northwestern Ohio with approximately 4,500 students from across the USA and several foreign countries. Today

UNOH features the colleges of Applied Technologies, Business, Occupational Professions and Health Professions in addition to graduate-school programs.

As for the school's athletic roots, for a period from the late '70s through the mid '80s, NBC Tech fielded men's and women's basketball teams nicknamed the Eagles, but cost factors eventually forced a decision to eliminate those programs. Over the next three decades, however, the school changed dramatically, and by 2006, UNOH president, Dr. Jeffrey Jarvis, and his board of directors decided that implementing a comprehensive athletic program would not only create an important asset to campus life and the community in general but also would be an excellent way to produce additional student enrollment.

Chris Adams was hired in June, 2006, as the first athletic director and head men's basketball coach at UNOH, and one of his first recruits was yours truly. Over the lunch to which he invited me, he explained that the university was going to bring back a men's and women's basketball program in the 2007-08 school year. The long-range athletic plan, he continued, was to add women's volleyball in the fall of 2008, with men's and women's golf, tennis, soccer and bowling, plus baseball and softball all to come shortly thereafter. Since I was no longer involved in high-school sports broadcasting, he wanted me to consider becoming the play-by-play voice of UNOH athletics.

Now, my first reaction was negative because I had just left a full-time sports broadcasting job for the less-stressful life of retirement. But my thought process changed when Chris assured me that I would not be required to travel. UNOH's primary interest was internet coverage of their home games with a chance that some of them would also air simultaneously on local radio. Given those parameters, I told Chris that I would consider the long-range implications of this kind of commitment, and if interested, submit a proposal to him outlining what I would need to accept his offer. There was no rush because the first home basketball game at UNOH was still more than a year away.

After talking it over with Amy, I concluded that this was an ideal opportunity to continue doing play-by-play and to earn some money to help offset the cost of the extra traveling we wanted to do in retirement. College-level talent promised interesting games to broadcast and, by being required to do only home games, I could weave most personal travel plans into the times the UNOH teams were on the road. My only stipulation regarding availability was to reserve the right to find someone else to do the broadcast if there was a home date that conflicted with a family-related commitment.

Chris and I had lunch again a couple of weeks later, and I gave him my proposal. He had no problem with the money I proposed, the equipment I wanted the school to purchase to provide a quality air product, or the possibility that I might miss a game or two during the season.

And so a deal was struck. From the initial broadcasts of men's and women's home basketball games in 2007-08, my involvement has grown to airing home volleyball matches in the fall and to doing home baseball and softball games in the spring.

Once the school made the commitment to an extensive athletic program, the need arose for a team name. So, a campus-wide survey was sent out requesting suggestions for a mascot. The nickname "Racers" was the ultimate choice, in large part because UNOH has a working partnership with NASCAR, owns and operates Limaland Motor Speedway in Elida, and because the university is so widely known for its auto-diesel mechanics curriculum.

After accepting the offer to become the play-by-play voice of the Racers, I began my search for color analysts for the various sports. Deb Schenk has been my sidekick in volleyball. Deb teaches at Lima Central Catholic, is a certified volleyball official, and coached the sport several years ago at LCC.

When the baseball and softball programs hit full stride and doubleheaders were the mainstay of the home schedule, Aaron Matthews, an air personality and play-by-play man for Childers Media Group (CMG) in Lima, joined me to share the workload in the press box. A number of those games have been carried by 93.1 The Fan, the ESPN affiliate in the CMG station lineup.

In basketball, my first UNOH color analyst was Matt
Metzger, a man who had played for Chris Adams at Elida High
School before playing college basketball at Ohio Northern
University in nearby Ada, Ohio. Matt works full time as a financial
analyst in a local company, Metzger Financial Services, started
by his father, Lynn. After a couple of years helping me with the
broadcasts, Matt agreed to join his former high school mentor as
an assistant coach with the UNOH men's basketball team, so he
traded his press-box chair for a seat on the bench on game days,
which left me in need of another color analyst.

I was fortunate because veteran LCC basketball coach Bob
Seggerson had recently retired, so he became my first choice to
take Matt's place on the UNOH broadcasts. I was thrilled when
he accepted the offer, and working with Segg for the last three
seasons has been one of the highlights of my career. Not only
has he been a close personal friend for more than thirty years
but his basketball knowledge is encyclopedic. Additionally, he
has developed an excellent knack for analyzing game situations
succinctly and communicating that information to our listeners in
a knowledgeable and entertaining way without disrupting the flow
of my play-by-play, which any broadcaster will tell you is vital to a
quality product. And, because a number of the UNOH games each
season are carried locally either on 93.1 The Fan or on WIMA,
area fans who watched Segg coach for three decades now get to
hear his basketball expertise first hand on the radio.

UNOH initially joined the American Mideast Conference,
but after two years decided to become a member of the more
competitive NAIA Division II Wolverine-Hoosier Athletic
Conference (WHAC). That decision followed a commitment
by Dr. Jarvis and the board of directors to initiate an aggressive
building program to provide first-class athletic facilities as soon as
possible.

Many of those facilities are already in place. Over the past
seven years, the university has built tennis courts, a soccer pitch,
and baseball and softball venues complete with locker rooms,
coaches' offices, and press boxes. To help support the more

than four hundred athletes now on campus, the university also purchased a vacated Office Depot store directly across Cable Road from the main administration building, gutted it, and transformed it into a first-class indoor athletic training facility not only for UNOH athletes but also for the student body and faculty.

While the Racers still play basketball and volleyball in the same facility that the NBC Tech Eagles used thirty-five years ago, financing for a new arena is being sought and hopes are that this final piece to the UNOH athletic-facility puzzle will be in place well before the end of this decade. When all is said and done, UNOH will have invested between fifteen and twenty million dollars in athletic infrastructure.

To say that I have enjoyed my post-WIMA radio jobs is an understatement. Between my work as Northwest Conference commissioner and my association with UNOH, I was able to create for myself a nearly perfect daily balance. Whenever someone has asked how I like retirement, my standard response has always been, "I highly recommend it! I always have something I can do… but seldom have anything I have to do."

To paraphrase the words of former Cincinnati Reds pitcher and broadcaster, Joe Nuxhall, I'm rounding third and heading for home on this written journey through my seventy-plus years on this planet, but, some very important final thoughts are in order before I cross home plate.

All In The Family

When I stop to thank the Lord each day for the blessings in my life, I have many to consider, not the least of which is a complex yet so very fulfilling journey of faith, one that has produced both a deep and strong relationship with Jesus Christ and also a wonderful sense of peace and tranquility as I inch closer to life's finish line.

The blessings bestowed upon me are many. I was raised in a great family and realize that I was the beneficiary of an excellent high school and college education. Additionally, I also felt privileged to serve my country in the U.S. Navy. I discovered an interest in and a talent for sports broadcasting and was able to turn that combination into an enjoyable and profitable career. I experienced the joy of fathering two natural children and was blessed also to have a stepson, and they have, in turn, given me six beautiful grandchildren. And, I have survived more than seventy years with no major health problems.

The death of my biological mother at age fourteen was very difficult, but my father's courage and tenacity in the face of such a tragedy set a tremendous example for me and my siblings. His subsequent marriage to Anne, the woman we've called mom since 1959, was well into its thirty-eighth year when he lost his battle with pancreatic cancer on December 31, 1996.

During the final third of his seventy-nine years on this earth, Robert J. Mullen forged an impressive second career. After retiring from government service at age fifty-four, he returned to school and pursued a life-long interest in art history. He earned the first Ph.D. offered by the art department at the University of Maryland in 1971.

The Mullen family eventually moved from Silver Spring, Maryland to San Antonio, Texas where dad became a professor of art history at the San Antonio branch of the University of Texas (UTSA). Over the next twenty years, he made many forays into the Oaxaca area of Mexico and became one of this country's foremost authorities on Mexican church architecture.

During the final ten years of his life, he wrote three detailed and scholarly research books on that subject (*Dominican Architecture in Sixteenth-Century Oaxaca*, *The Architecture and Sculpture of Oaxaca, 1530s-1980s*, and *Architecture and Its Sculpture in Viceregal Mexico*). Upon his retirement from UTSA he donated more than 20,000 slides on the subject to the school's library.

About five years after my dad passed away, mom chose to remarry. Richard Smith was a widower she knew from church. The union paired the mother of seven girls and three boys with the father of seven boys and one girl and has been a great blessing to both of them for the past thirteen years.

Although my first wife, Rosemary, and I parted ways in our mid-thirties, we have been fortunate to maintain a cordial relationship through the years, and her devotion as a mother to our daughter and son has been unwavering and much appreciated.

But, when it comes to earthly blessings, my list starts with the night in April, 1980, when Kathy Stewart introduced me to the woman with whom I have now shared nearly half my life. And, as of this writing, as Amy and I enjoy our thirty-fourth year together, the favorite "insider" phrase we use, coupled with a light fist bump, to describe our relationship is, "We're a team!" Certainly, no description could be more accurate.

To be sure, there was instant chemistry between us, so much so that a number of friends cautioned that this was, at least in my case, perhaps just an "on-the-rebound" emotional reaction. Amy had been divorced for about a year at the time we met, so her marital status was clear, but it had been only a few weeks since my separation from Rosemary.

Although I was certain that relationship was over, Amy was initially wary about my having second thoughts because of the children and was, therefore, somewhat hesitant about becoming too involved with me too quickly since my official divorce proceedings were still months from completion.

As spring morphed into summer and summer gave way to fall, we learned that we complemented each other in many ways and that our temperaments were well matched. We each had strengths in areas where the other was not as strong, and I grew to appreciate the fact that we had many similar interests and that we shared a balanced approach to our relationship. Right from the start we understood and respected the importance of "your time," "my time" and "our time" in the formula of successful day-to-day living.

As the rest of the year played out, Amy and I knew that we wanted to marry, so after my divorce became final in December, 1980, we set a wedding date for April 18, 1981. For reasons soon understood, the ceremony took place not in Lima but at South Park United Methodist Church in Dayton, Ohio, and was officiated by the pastor of that church, Reverend Lenn Geiger.

Amy Elaine Pearson was born in Lima to Charles and Elsie Pearson and grew up in the Methodist faith, first at Grace Methodist Church on Kibby Street in Lima, and then at Forest Park United Methodist Church on Lima's east side. Her childhood home from school age on was in the Lost Creek area on the same side of town. Forest Park remained Amy's home church during her first marriage and following her divorce.

Amy went through the Bath school system and spent a couple

of semesters at Bowling Green State University before marrying another Lima native, David Freel. Their son, Troy, was born March 3, 1969, and had just turned eleven at the time when I arrived on the scene.

After Amy and I met, and wanting to respect each other's religious backgrounds, she agreed to come with me to Catholic mass on some Sundays and I, in turn, attended Forest Park with her on other Sundays. After several times at mass, it was apparent that Amy was not comfortable with the ritual of the Catholic service and got little spiritual uplift from the experience. I, on the other hand, found Forest Park to be both welcoming on a personal basis and meaningful in terms of the religious message I was receiving.

Since I had struggled with some issues regarding the Catholic Church for a couple of years prior to meeting Amy, and given the respective experiences of our shared Sunday church explorations, I eventually decided to join her and worship permanently at Forest Park. In retrospect, it was one of the better decisions of my life because, more than thirty years later, I now attribute most of the steady growth in my Christian faith to my experience with the wonderful people and pastors who have made up the Forest Park Body of Christ.

When it came time for Amy and I to marry, she wanted a favorite former pastor at Forest Park, Lenn Geiger, to perform the ceremony so that meant planning our wedding at Reverend Geiger's current church in Dayton.

Since this was a second marriage for both of us, by design, only eleven people were present at the Saturday morning wedding in the South Park UMC chapel. Joining Reverend Geiger and the bride and groom were our three children; my sister, Pat Murphy, and her husband, Mike; and three close friends, Jane Weber and Alta and Doug Heintz.

Following the ceremony, we returned to Lima, where Amy and I hosted a small afternoon reception at a place that no longer exists but at the time was one of the most popular restaurants in Lima, the Buckingham Inn on Elida Road. While the day included very little in the way of pomp and circumstance, the events of April

18, 1981, were a beautiful and memorable way to start the second half of our lives.

One of our early discoveries as a couple was a mutual desire to travel, so, to enhance the opportunity to see the country and beyond its borders given the financial responsibilities of our blended family, we decided to forego all gift giving to each other for birthdays, anniversaries, Christmas or other special days and put any spare money that would have gone for those gifts into a travel fund.

During our more than three decades together, our favorite way to travel has been cruise vacations to almost every part of the world. Amy and I have cruised in the Mediterranean and also the Baltic, off Alaska, all over the Caribbean, past the Mexican Riviera, through the Panama Canal, off South America and around the British Isles, and off Hawaii and Australia and New Zealand as well, and we still have a few more places on our cruise bucket list.

During the period from 1984 through 1993, we worked with WIMA Radio and a good friend and local travel agent, Chris Seddelmeyer, to design "Follow-the-Reds" trips all over the United States. Since our station carried the Cincinnati Reds broadcasts, we combined a couple of Reds road games with a variety of other sightseeing experiences and built nice one-week escorted summer vacation trips to offer the general public. Much of our own travel expense on these trips was covered in exchange for the work we did during the week coordinating the transportation and schedule of activities for the Reds fans that joined us.

In all, we took eight "Follow-the-Reds" trips with group sizes ranging from thirteen to forty-three people. A few of those people traveled with us several times and remain good friends twenty years later. These trips were possible to organize because prior to 1994, airlines permitted a travel agent to reserve a block of seats months in advance with no payment required until thirty days prior to departure. This gave us the opportunity to cost out and prepare a vacation package, sell it to the public, and then simply turn back any unneeded seats to the airline just before the thirty-day mark for final settlement and confirmation.

At the beginning of 1994, the entire airline industry changed to its current procedure of requiring traveler names and full payment at the time of booking any future flight. Since we were in no position to pay for a couple of dozen round-trip airline tickets in advance and then hope to sell enough packages to recoup our money, that form of summer vacation came to an end after the final trip in June, 1993, to see the Reds play the Rockies in Denver, with a side visit to the ski resort at Vail, Colorado.

Over the years, Amy and I have been fortunate to travel with several special local couples. In the early years, we took some great trips with Gene and Iona Hamilton and Jeff and Linda Prince. For the past seventeen years, we have enjoyed long-weekend getaways each October with Richard and Ann Warren to places all over the United States and Canada. And, we've also cruised several times and shared home visits with Bob and Candy Ferguson from Denver, a couple we met on a cruise to the Mexican Riviera.

If one were to step into the office area of our home, he or she would see attached to one wall a large piece of specially made sheet metal that contains nearly 250 magnets that represent all the places we have visited during our travels. The magnet collection has provided a handy, comprehensive and relatively inexpensive way to remember the wonderful times Amy and I have shared doing something we both enjoy so much, seeing the exquisite beauty of God's creations all over the world.

From the very beginning, Amy understood the nature of my work and fully supported the many nights I spent away from home broadcasting ballgames. While she was a big Ohio State and Cincinnati Reds fan, her interest in high school sports was limited to a few local rivalry games each year so she was content, for the most part, to stay home or do something with a girlfriend on game nights.

When we were together in a public setting, Amy was sometimes asked during general conversation, "Do you go with Mike to the games when he broadcasts?" Her standard response that always brought a chuckle was, "No. He doesn't go to work with me, so I don't go to work with him!" After I stopped doing high school play-by-play and moved on to UNOH broadcasts, Amy began to enjoy coming to Racer volleyball and basketball games and now often joins me on those evenings.

While I was busy with broadcasting and sales duties at WIMA, Amy was moving steadily forward on her own career path. When we met, she was the employment supervisor at Continental Plastics on Reservoir Road in Lima. She had been chosen in 1975 by the plant manager, Trevor Evans, as the first local person to join the facility's start-up team and was tasked with hiring shift workers whose job was to produce a variety of plastic containers for Procter and Gamble's liquid detergent and fabric softener plant located less than a mile away.

After about ten years at Continental Plastics, the chance for a higher-paying job surfaced when an acquaintance Amy knew through membership in the Lima Personnel Association recruited her for the position of benefits coordinator at Excello in Lima, a plant that manufactured blades for jet engines and later became Airfoil Textron. Although she was not actively seeking a job change, she could not turn down this chance for career advancement and began the new position in November, 1985.

Roughly eight years later, the results of union contract negotiations at Airfoil Textron in 1993 led to a corporate decision eventually to move the Lima operation to a non-union setting in Thomasville, Georgia. Seeing the writing on the wall and not wishing to move south to keep her job, Amy took part in the first round of company layoffs in order to help her chances of finding another job in Lima.

It took the better part of year to accomplish, but in late 1994, Amy finally secured a claims position at the Ohio Bureau of Workers' Compensation (BWC) office in Lima. As a veteran of nearly twenty years in industry working on the employer's side of the state's compensation system for injured workers, she began her job with an advantage over most new BWC employees. After a couple of years in the claims department, she applied for and was promoted to a position as an employer service specialist.

This new responsibility allowed Amy to call on businesses

in three area counties and help their management find the most
cost-effective and efficient ways to navigate the labyrinth of BWC
rules and regulations. Many company owners and human resource
managers greatly appreciated working with Amy because she was
someone who had been in their shoes and understood their needs
and was not just another government bureaucrat trying to increase
their already-burdensome paperwork requirements. I imagine
that her clients were sad to see her retire from the workforce in
December, 2007.

I am a firm believer that all things in life happen for a
reason. A large part of the energy and effort I put into my career
was fueled by Amy's unconditional love and support. That our
lives intersected when they did and that we can now look back
together over more than three decades, two successful careers and
a wonderful family of three children and six grandchildren, I count
as my greatest blessing.

I mentioned that Troy had just turned eleven when Amy
and I met. My son Jeff was six months older than Troy, and Julie
was thirteen. All of them are now in their mid-forties, but they are
located far apart, and their lives are so busy that getting the whole
family together at the same time is quite challenging.

After high school, Julie spent her first semester of college
at Ohio University in Athens, Ohio, but at mid-year, decided the
location was too remote for her tastes, so she transferred to Ohio
State.

Julie was one of the many of her generation who grew up in
Lima, left for college, and never returned. She stayed in Columbus
after graduating from Ohio State and married Andy George in
1993. Victoria (Tori) George was born June 21, 1996, and Andrew
(Drew) George followed on December 12, 1997.

Julie and Andy divorced in 1999 and in April of 2001, she
married Bryan O'Donnell. It was a first marriage for Bryan, who
worked out of his own home in the Worthington Kilbourne school
district in Columbus. Following the wedding, Julie and the kids
moved in and have lived there ever since.

When her children were small, Julie started a business called

Sitters Unlimited. She recruited and vetted a group of mostly college students who had wide varieties of course schedules and wanted to use babysitting as a means to help put themselves through school. She then advertised her business in Columbus and, for a fee, provided a qualified sitter at any time, day or evening, for those in need of such a service.

Sitters Unlimited did quite well for several years and enabled Julie to be a stay-at-home mom, but it was a very labor-intensive business requiring an extensive amount of time on the telephone. After several years, that burden was eased when Julie had a business website built to enable most sitter requests, sitter assignments and billing to be done on-line.

However, when the economy took a downturn in 2009-10, Columbus families had less expendable income, so her business gradually slowed. Since Tori and Drew were older and no longer required constant supervision, Julie eventually elected to sell Sitters Unlimited and take a full-time job in the Worthington Kilbourne school system.

Jeff's adult life has been largely centered around one word – coaching. Playing both football and baseball at Lima Senior High School, Jeff was recruited to play football at Wittenberg University in Springfield, Ohio. After four years with the Tigers and earning small college All-American honors as a defensive back in his senior year, Jeff graduated from Wittenberg in 1990 and took a job as a management trainee for the Foot Locker chain of athletic-shoe stores. He wanted to get into college coaching, but that was much easier said than done, so he supported himself after college through the job with Foot Locker. He also received a small stipend for helping to coach football at Hamilton Township High School in suburban Columbus during the 1990 season.

Jeff's big break came in the summer of 1991 when a former standout player at Wittenberg in the late sixties, Bob Wagner, who was then head football coach at the University of Hawaii, had a graduate assistant coach from California quit his job unexpectedly just three weeks before fall practice started in Honolulu.

With little time to sift through a file drawer full of

applications, and wanting to help out a Wittenberg football player if possible, Wagner called the football department at the school and asked if they could recommend anyone for a graduate assistant's position who would be available on short notice. Knowing Jeff's desire to get into college coaching, the Wittenberg staff told Bob Wagner they knew the perfect man for the job.

So, on a July evening in 1991, Jeff received a totally unexpected phone call from the head coach at the University of Hawaii and was offered a graduate assistant position on a Division I football staff. The rest, as they say, is history.

Jeff immediately resigned from Foot Locker and shortly thereafter flew to Honolulu where he spent the 1991 season doing whatever his head coach needed him to do. With almost no money and living conditions that included sleeping on an office couch and eating at the football training table, Jeff, despite what many would view as a rather Spartan lifestyle, enjoyed the experience in Hawaii but also looked for any chance to get back to Ohio.

With his foot now in the door of college coaching and something official to put on his resume, Jeff was now ready to make a move. One of his former assistant coaches at Wittenberg who had since joined the staff at Ohio University arranged for Jeff to return to the mainland in 1992 for a similar graduate assistant's job with the Bobcats.

During the next three years, Jeff served in that position at OU and earned a master's degree in sports administration. He also met his future wife, Andrea Rami, an OU student who had played high school basketball in the Cleveland suburb of Berea. They married in 1995 and produced three beautiful children over the next six years.

Nathan (Nate) Mullen arrived on March 24, 1996. Daughter Rami joined the family on June 17, 2000, and her sister Margaret (Maggie) followed on July 9, 2001. With Jeff's first daughter, her name comes with a history. Rami's first name is also her mother's maiden name. Andrea was the youngest of six children and had lost her father shortly before she and Jeff married. When she and Jeff were searching for a name for their first daughter, they chose

Rami as a beautiful way to perpetuate Andrea's family name in the Mullen clan.

After one season under new Ohio University head coach, Jim Grobe, in 1995, Jeff was promoted to a full-time assistant coach and then, in 2000, moved his family to Winston-Salem, North Carolina, when Grobe accepted the head coaching job at Wake Forest University.

Jeff spent seven years coaching quarterbacks for the Deacons, including former Kenton High School standout, Ben Mauk, and then landed the job as offensive coordinator at West Virginia in 2007 when Bill Stewart took over as head coach of the Mountaineers following the unexpected departure of Rich Rodriguez to Michigan.

Jeff had absolutely no connection to West Virginia, but Bill Stewart and Jim Grobe were longtime coaching friends. So, when Stewart called his buddy asking for a recommendation for an offensive coordinator, Grobe gave him Jeff's name and said he was ready to make that move. After just one interview with Coach Stewart, Jeff was offered the job and took control of the Mountaineers' high-powered offense.

Despite three 9-3 seasons in Morgantown and three straight bowl appearances, when a new athletic director, Oliver Luck, arrived at West Virginia, he decided to change head coaches so Jeff and the rest of the staff were out of a job following the 2009 campaign.

In March of 2010, a coaching friend of Jeff's from his days at Wake Forest, Brad Lambert, was chosen to start a brand new Division I football program at UNC-Charlotte. Lambert's background was on the defensive side of the football, so one of his first decisions was to hire Jeff to run his offense. Everyone in the Mullen family was thrilled to have a new coaching opportunity and also happy to be moving back to a milder climate in North Carolina.

Charlotte's athletic nickname happens to be the 49ers, so I had a great deal of fun when people asked if Jeff had found a new job following his departure from West Virginia. I would say, "He sure has. He's the new offensive coordinator of the 49ers!" After allowing the stunned look to remain on their face for a couple of seconds, I smiled and explained that his new position had nothing to do with San Francisco or the NFL.

After two years of recruiting and watching the completion of a new stadium and football facilities on the Charlotte campus, Jeff's 49ers played their first full season in 2013 against Football Championship Subdivision (FCS) competition, which are schools that used to be classified 1-AA by the NCAA. After one more season at that level in 2014, the 49ers will face a full Football Bowl Subdivision (FBS) Division I schedule as a member of Conference USA in 2015.

While Julie preferred a big school like Ohio State and Jeff enjoyed the much smaller campus at Wittenberg, Troy opted for a university sized somewhere in between. Following his graduation from Shawnee High School in 1987, Troy enrolled at the University of Cincinnati, where he completed a degree in economics four years later.

Shortly after college, a mutual friend got him a job handling insurance claims for a small company in Cincinnati. Troy eventually accepted a position with a much larger firm in the Queen City, Great American Insurance, the company that bought the stadium naming rights when the Cincinnati Reds left Riverfront Stadium and moved into Great American Ball Park in 2003.

Troy did very well at Great American and continually took on-line classes to expand his level of insurance certification and raise his value within the company. Much of his work required him to interact on the phone with agents from smaller insurance companies whose policies were underwritten by Great American. One of those agents was Jennifer (Jenn) Devaney, who worked for a small company in New Jersey that specialized in travel insurance.

After many phone conversations, Troy and Jenn finally met in person when she came to Cincinnati for a training seminar, and the relationship that had started on the telephone quickly grew into something serious. Before long, Troy told us he was planning to quit his job in Cincinnati and move to New Jersey to marry Jenn.

Since she was the youngest of five children in a very close-knit family, she didn't want to leave her surroundings and move to Ohio, so he was going to look for a new insurance job there and move to the East Coast. The wedding took place in fall of 2003, and our sixth grandchild, Liam Freel, joined the family on March 6, 2006. Troy continues to work in the insurance industry.

Once Amy and I became grandparents, we had to decide on what we wanted our grandkids to call us. Because there were more than the usual number of grandparents involved in our extended family, we wanted to choose names that would not conflict with others in that category.

For myself, I chose the name "Pops" for two reasons. First, I liked the sound of it and felt it suited my personality. Second, since Jeff's wife, Andrea, had recently lost her father, I thought it was a name she as well as her kids could comfortably call me.

For Amy, even though there were only three letters in her name, a number of her friends had phonetically shortened it to "Aim" so she opted for "Gramaim," a fused one-syllable version of "Grandma Amy." As the years went by, that morphed into the initials, GA, so now we're known throughout the family as simply Pops and GA.

Watching our grandchildren grow up has been a wonderful experience. Although none has ever lived in Lima, Amy and I have and will continue to see them as often as possible. Our road trips to their homes have become a vital and fulfilling part of retirement life. As of this writing the six range in age from 8 to 18, and their journeys thus far have touched every level of the emotional spectrum, from the highest of highs to the lowest of lows.

Hockey is an extremely popular sport in New Jersey, so our youngest grandchild, Liam, learned to skate before he was three and has been involved in organized hockey programs ever since. He's a walking encyclopedia of National Hockey League teams and players, and he's also a big baseball fan who roots for the Yankees in the American League and the Reds in the National League. And, as I write this story, Liam is a bright, sports-loving and active eight-year-old who dons goaltending equipment during hockey season and catcher's equipment during baseball season.

Jeff's three kids have also focused on athletics as their major extra-curricular activity. Nate is a carbon copy of his father with a special talent for football. He is already a two-time all-conference slot receiver and kick/punt returner at Hickory Ridge High School and is a 2014 pre-season all-state selection in North Carolina's Division 3-A as he enters his senior year. Nate recently made a verbal commitment to accept a Division I college football scholarship from UNC-Charlotte, so Pops and GA will get to watch their son coach and their grandson play for the same team over the next several years.

Rami and Maggie have made volleyball their sport of choice and are both talented players. Rami enters ninth grade in the fall of 2014 and hopes to see action as a setter on either the JV or Varsity volleyball team at Hickory Ridge. Maggie will enter eighth grade and play for the middle school volleyball team.

As for Julie's two children, Tori recently graduated from Worthington Kilbourne High School in Columbus and will begin her freshman year at the University of Kentucky in the fall of 2014. Tori's forte through high school was music and theater. She has been blessed with amazing vocal talent and was a member of a city-wide choir from the sixth grade on as well as several high school choral groups. She played significant roles in all of the school musicals, and was one of the field commanders for the Kilbourne marching band her senior year after previously playing clarinet in the same band.

Drew has loved athletics since the time he could walk. He's been very active in soccer, basketball and baseball his whole life. He is a huge Ohio State fan and has a goal of someday playing baseball for the Buckeyes. The mere fact that such a goal is within the realm of possibility is a miracle.

On November 7, 2013, Drew went to the doctor because he had been feeling unusually tired for several weeks. After tests for mononucleosis proved negative, his family doctor directed him to Nationwide Children's Hospital in Columbus for more tests. That evening, doctors informed Julie that her son had a rare form of acute myeloid leukemia (AML) and, in that instant, life changed dramatically for the entire family.

From November 7, 2013 to May 7, 2014, Drew spent all but three weeks in the hospital fighting for his life. His only realistic chance for survival was to find a suitable donor for a bone-marrow transplant. By the grace of God, his only sibling, Tori, turned out to be a perfect donor match.

After multiple rounds of chemotherapy, countless prayers, and an incredible showing of community support for the family, Tori donated her bone marrow on April 9, 2014, and it was transplanted into Drew the same day.

For the next three weeks, Drew was a very sick young man as his sixteen-year-old body tried to fight off the "foreign" substance, but fortunately, Tori's marrow grafted beautifully and that battle was won. And then came the sweetest words a parent or grandparent in such circumstance could possibly hear. Drew was pronounced cancer-free. On May 7, 2014, he was allowed to come home six months to the day after he had been diagnosed with AML. His bone marrow now registers 98.5 percent Tori's cells, and he has, as we all do, every hope of enjoying a long and productive life.

Because he has a whole new immune system and cannot yet risk being in large crowds, Drew will not be able to return to his junior year classes at Worthington Kilbourne until sometime in early 2015, but he will be able to keep up with his studies through tutors and on-line work. Also, the doctor has put Drew's Ohio State baseball dream back in play by telling him that he will be able to rejoin his high school team in the spring of 2015.

Praise the Lord that Drew's six-month nightmare is over and that he is on the road to a full recovery. Because the leukemia compromised his immune system, his inability to fight infection meant that very few people could actually be in the room with him during his long hospital stay. His parents, Julie and Andy, and his maternal grandmother, Rosemary, spent countless hours at his side providing his family lifeline during the ordeal and can never be thanked enough for all they did.

Thanks also go to the wonderfully talented doctors and nurses at Nationwide Children's Hospital in Columbus and to the hundreds of friends and neighbors in the Worthington Kilbourne School District who helped Drew and the family cope with and eventually beat a very serious form of blood cancer.

And, of course, without his sister, Tori, and the gift of her bone marrow, Drew's story might have taken a much different turn. She is a life saver in the quintessential definition of that term, and for the rest of their lives they will share April 9 as a common second "birthday."

I can think of no better way to end the discourse of what has been my life's journey than to thank God for all of the many blessings that He has showered upon me.

And, what better time than now to use the words I used so very often to close out my high school broadcasts over the years:

"For John Barton and George Frazee, this is Mike Mullen wishing you all good night and good sports!"

EPILOGUE

When I started this effort to recap my life's journey, an expedition that included more than three decades at WIMA radio, my goal was to have a finished manuscript ready for print by the end of 2014. Thanks to the steady guidance and invaluable input from my friend and editor, John Grindrod, I will be able to reach that goal.

As I go forward, my plan is to continue as the play-by-play voice of UNOH athletics for as long as my health and their willingness to have me continue. I truly enjoy the part-time work and, with a new gymnasium in the plans over the next few years, I would love to broadcast at least one season in the new Racer facility before unplugging the microphone for the final time in my play-by-play career.

You've already met many people from my days at WIMA who were an integral part of my air work. I also want to acknowledge some other longtime co-workers and thank them for their support over the years.

First and foremost is Art Versnick, who started on the air, then went to sales, and finally succeeded Les Rau as the general manager of the station after Les retired. Art was always a strong proponent of local sports coverage and helped me succeed in many ways.

In the administrative area, people like Evelyn Austin, Robin Palmer, Carolyn Dalrymple, Polly Anderson, Claudia Kennel and Sheri Lybarger made my life a lot easier because of their support and the professional way they did their own jobs.

Two of the station's most widely recognized local talk-show hosts were Valaire Orchard and Dennis Shreefer. While they worked in different eras and their show content and approach were as diametrically opposed as possible, both became good friends and valued former co-workers. I especially want to thank Valaire for treating me like a second son, not only during our time together at WIMA but also into retirement as well.

There were literally dozens of air talents who entertained area listeners during my career. Bill Holden, Bob Nelson, Steve Lewis, Gordy Price, Mike Miller, Jeannie Haning, Kathy Hague, and Dave Woodward were those with whom I most interacted and each added a different variety of spice to life in radio.

I think the news department deserves a special mention. Longtime news director, Tom Watkins, was one of many that made WIMA news number one in the radio market for so many years. Tom was a no-nonsense reporter with a newspaper background who had contacts all over town and who earned their respect by the way he did his job. Others I worked with closely in the news department include Bob Ziegler, Neil Winget and Deb Duncan.

And, among those who made advertising sales their contribution to the company's success, Jim Coolahan, Paul Buzzard, Bob Torbet, Doreen Loretta, Juanita Brown, Teresa Silone, Chris Estes and Tom Krouse certainly have enriched my life on many levels.

And, so it has gone for me on my journey which, as it is for many, was filled at times with some uncertainties and trepidations before I found direction during my first broadcasts while in the Navy and ultimately, great fulfillment. Thanks again to the thousands of listeners who loyally followed my broadcasts and gave meaning to my efforts to bring an enjoyable local sports product to Lima and West Central Ohio. Forty-one years after arriving here, I now gladly call Lima home and, in retirement, feel a true sense of accomplishment and satisfaction and, of course, so very much of that is because of you.